MW01626048

Paule Vézelay

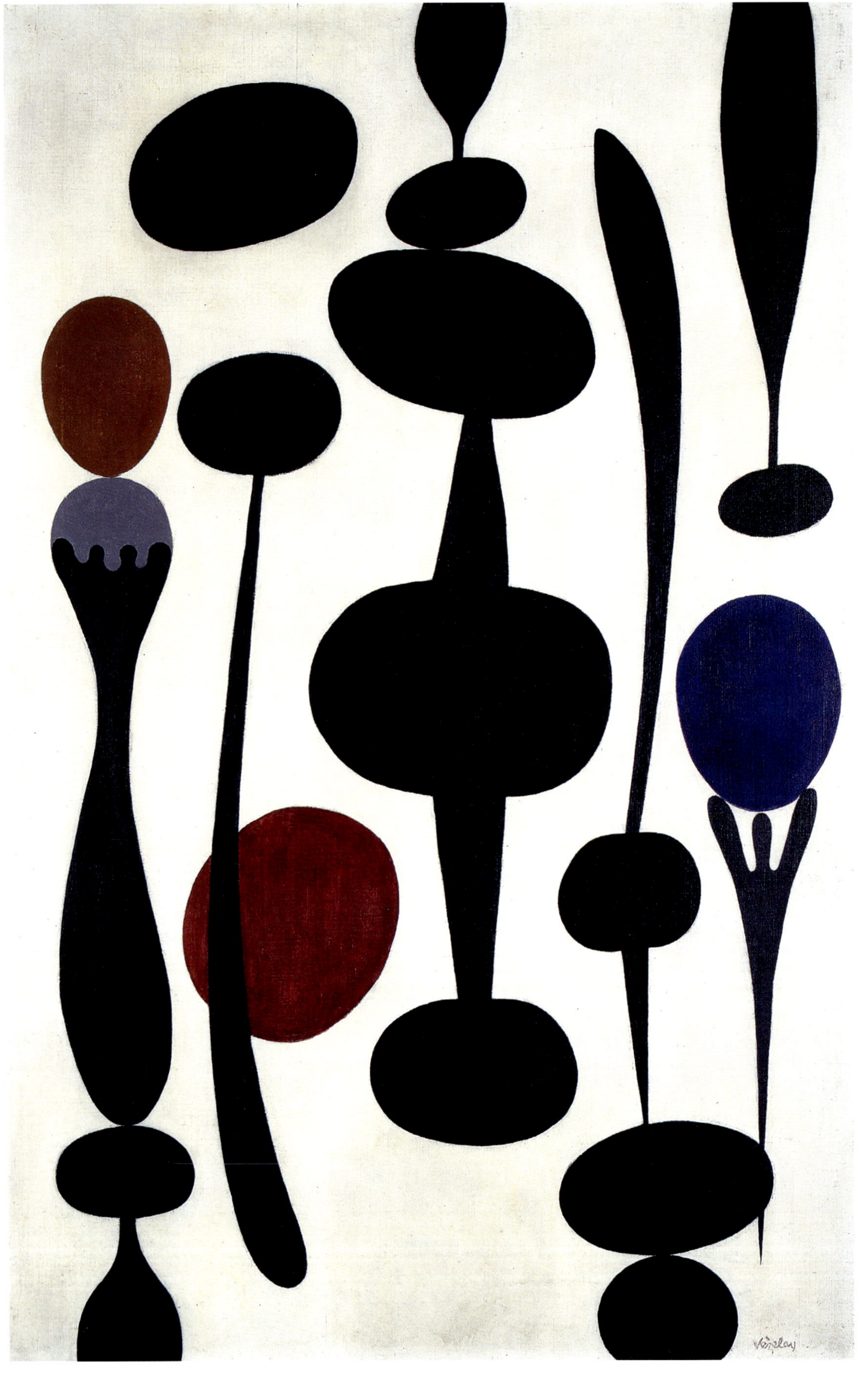

Edited by Simon Grant with contributions by
Gemma Brace, Nina Gioria, Helen Janecek and
Sarah Wilson, and a foreword by Sally Jarman

Paule Vézelay

Living Lines

LUND
HUMPHRIES

First published in 2025 by Lund Humphries

Lund Humphries
Huckletree Shoreditch
Alphabeta Building
18 Finsbury Square
London EC2A 1AH
UK

www.lundhumphries.com

Paule Vézelay: Living Lines

ISBN: 978-1-84822-704-0

A Cataloguing-in-Publication record for this book is available from the British Library

Designed by Mark Thomson
Set in LL Supreme
Printed in Bosnia and Herzegovina

Front cover image: *Growing Forms*, 1946, oil on canvas, 73 × 60 cm, private collection
Back cover image: *Self Portrait*, 1927, oil on canvas, 65.1 × 54.3 cm, National Portrait Gallery, London
p.2: *Silhouettes*, 1938, oil on canvas, 92 × 60 cm, private collection

This book is printed on sustainably sourced paper

Contents

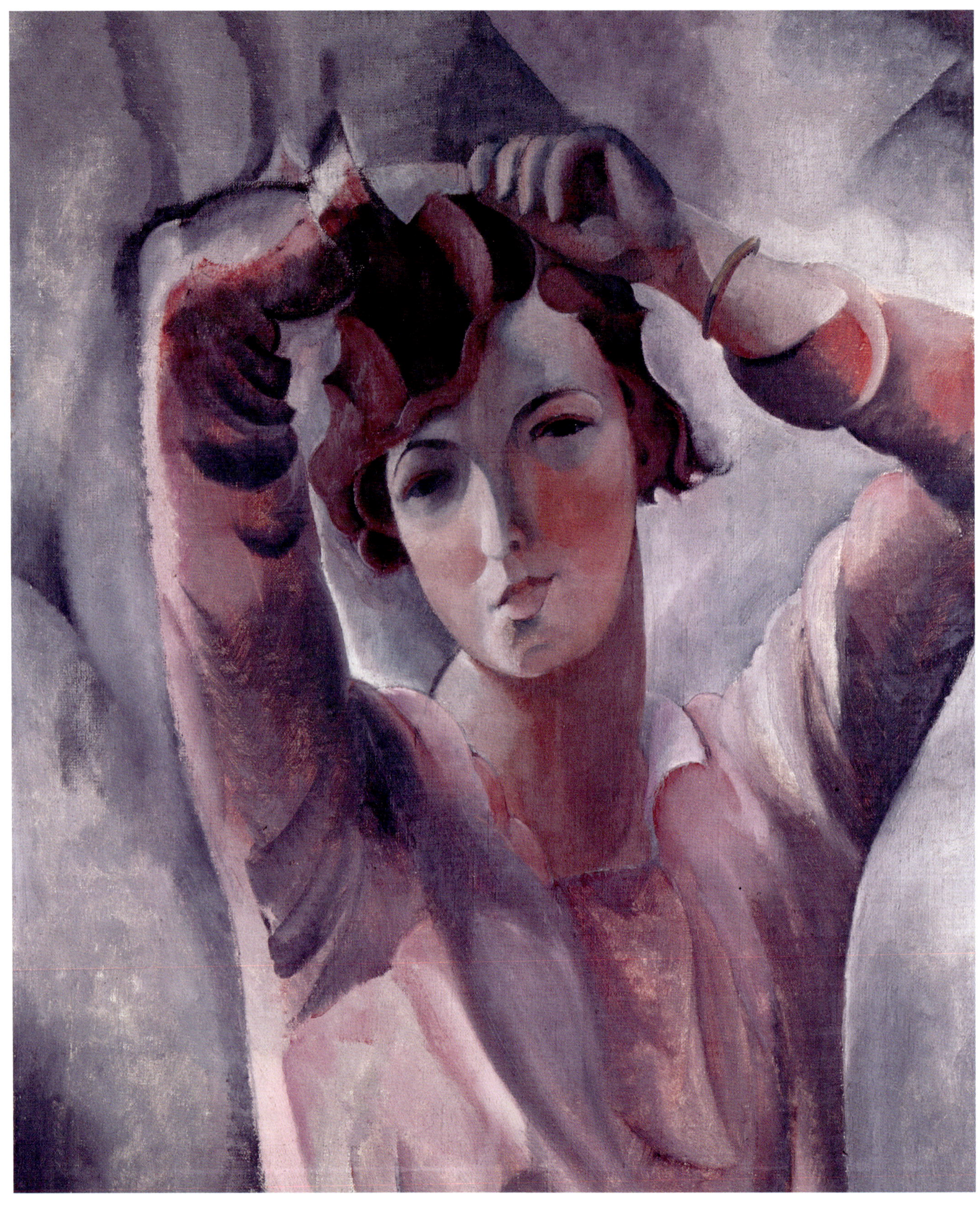

1
Paule Vézelay, *Self Portrait*, 1927, oil on canvas, 65.1 × 54.3 cm, National Portrait Gallery, London

Sally Jarman (1935–2023)

Foreword: My Aunt, Paule Vézelay

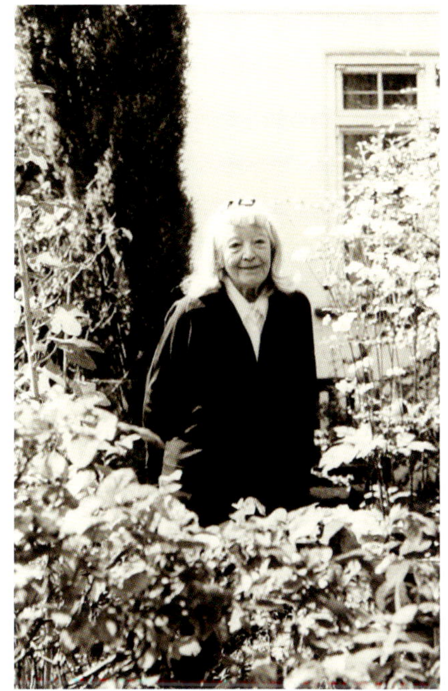

2
Paule Vézelay in her garden, Barnes, London, 1970s, photograph, Estate of Paule Vézelay

Paule was my aunt – my father Guthrie's older sister. Paule and Guthrie corresponded regularly, not about art but about investments, taxes, bad neighbours, central heating and fences. It was clear that the family were baffled by having an abstract artist in their midst and even more by someone who later changed her name. In 1964 Paule wrote to my husband, Christopher, saying, 'You must write to me as Paule' (not Marjorie), as she preferred not to be reminded of her maiden name 'Watson-Williams'. She also disliked any suggestion of being paraded as a woman artist.

When, as a child, I visited my grandparents in Bristol, I remember that Paule was not much in evidence. She would later tell me that she felt a disappointment to her mother, who had wanted her to be a traditional girl – arranging flowers and being a 'polished corner', as she put it. In addition, my grandparents had adopted her stepsister (also called Marjorie) . . . and I believe she may have displaced Paule as their main focus. Perhaps as a result, Paule was a very private person, and as soon as she started at Bristol School of Art she wanted to be a professional artist. This priority remained throughout her long life.

As an aunt she was always a very affectionate and faithful correspondent. She was generous, too, and would send collage cut-outs to my son Sam when he was quite young. She loved gardening, designing her own garden, and even sent some of her roses to my parents in Kathmandu. She was chic, with a flair for clothes, and always dressed smartly. She loved to entertain people with an especially artistic presentation of the food. She was often rather scathing about people who did not understand abstract art.

Why was she not better known during her life? The answer lies partly in herself. The art critic J.P. Hodin wrote to her in frustration saying, 'You are your own worst enemy.' Paule was both her own severest critic and yet sure of her position as 'Master of Classical Abstraction', as Hodin called her. Like Turner, whom she much admired, she came to think of her works as her own children and became reluctant to part with them at any price. She was too genteel and of the wrong generation to market her art. She preserved a dignified, unworldly integrity. For over 40 years she kept the innovative faith of 1930s Paris alive in her London studio.

I regret not having had more discussion with her about art. I was working part-time and bringing up two sons, which meant that we did not meet as often as we might have, though we occasionally went to Barnes to tackle her overgrown garden. Despite all that, I came to love her work and to be very proud of her achievements.

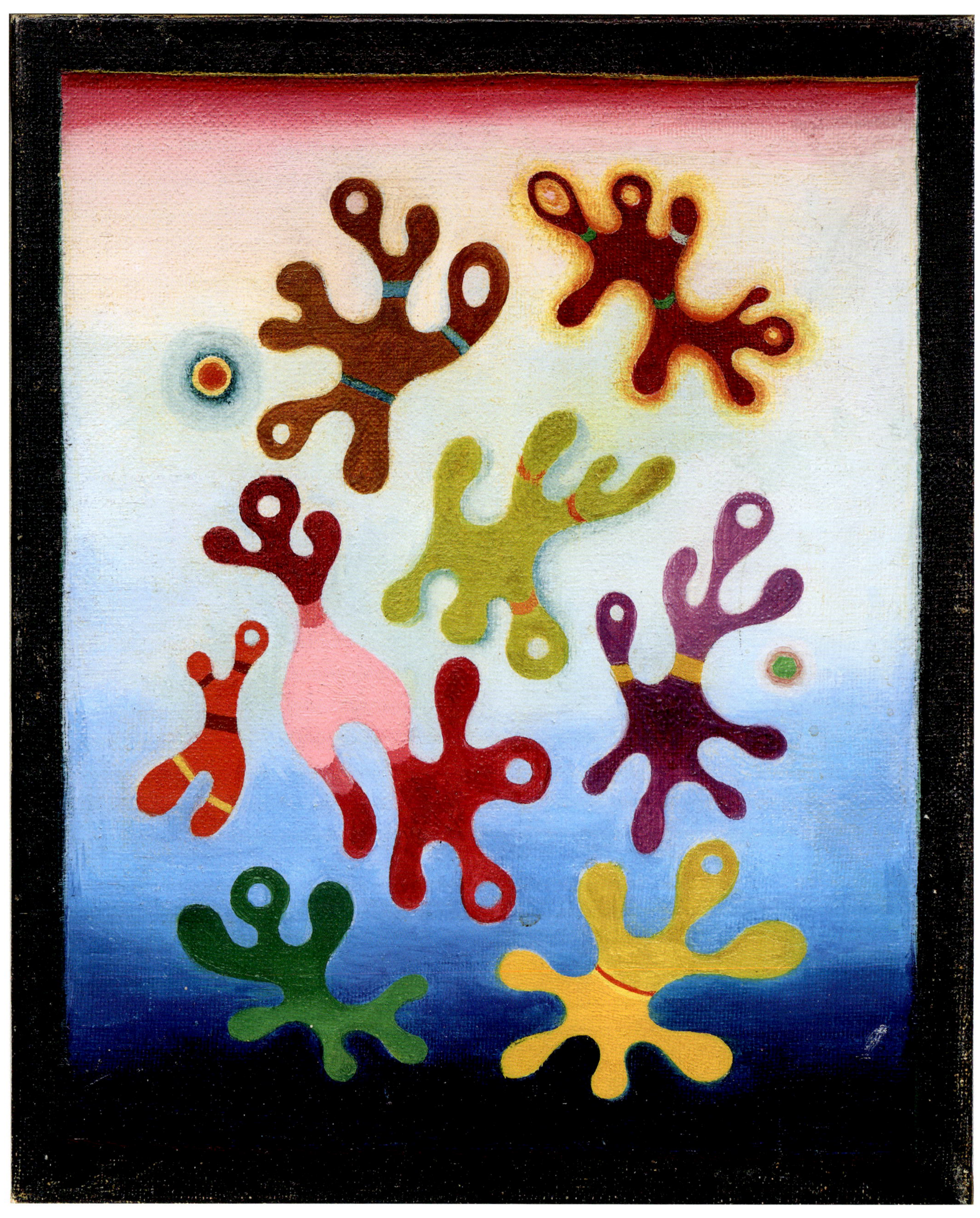

3
Paule Vézelay, *Eight Curved Forms and Two Circles*,
1946, oil on canvas, 30 × 25 cm, private collection

Simon Grant

Introduction

In the hot summer of 1983 Ronald Alley, Keeper of the Modern Collection at the Tate Gallery, London, was guiding a well-dressed elderly lady among the guests of the Queen's annual garden party at Buckingham Palace. Most would not recognise the 90-year-old artist Paule Vézelay (née Marjorie Watson-Williams), who was enjoying the critical acclaim for her retrospective at the Tate several months earlier. It had been a long time coming for the Bristol-born woman who had resiliently navigated her own path through much of the 20th century.

Despite Vézelay's art being exhibited widely and regularly from the 1920s until her death, this is the first book on the artist to introduce her life and work. Over her long career she would create an extraordinarily diverse output, encompassing painting, collage, sculpture, constructions, illustration, textiles, photography, poetry, prose, critical writing and even a film script. This publication focuses primarily on her early years in Paris, from the 1920s through to the outbreak of the Second World War, during which time her work moved from figuration to abstraction, for which she would become best known. The book also brings to light, for the first time in detail, her little-known success as a designer of textiles, produced during her later decades while living in London.

The book aims to show how Vézelay became a formidable presence in the International avant-garde scene in Paris during the 1930s, where she could count among her friends many of the great artists of the day, including Sophie Taeuber-Arp, Jean Arp, Marlow Moss, Wassily Kandinsky and André Masson. It also shows how Vézelay can be regarded as one of the first English abstract artists (along with Moss), with an abstract drawing, dating from 1928, made several years before Barbara Hepworth, Ben Nicholson and Henry Moore moved to abstraction.

Vézelay knew that it was Paris where she needed to be. As Sarah Wilson writes (p.77), Paris offered an opportunity for 'self-fashioning, self-reinvention, linked with place, time and remarkable encounters', leaving behind England's parochial art scene and its male-dominated art establishment. In terms of her art, she would be most dedicated to an exploration of line, something that she connected to the 'language of the artist since primitive man'.[1] From her early Beardsley-esque illustrations and her figurative Parisian circus and restaurant scenes, her serpentine lines would transform into imagined abstractions, most notably her boxed constructions made with wire or fishing line stretched, and sometimes intertwined, across the picture plane. Yet, for Vézelay, such innovation would also extend beyond rational enquiry. As Gemma Brace notes (p.31), Vézelay bestowed a form of divine destiny upon the simple line, believing that such lines had an 'almost celestial quality which miraculously imbues them with "Life"'.[2]

When asked by Germaine Greer 'Why do curves appear in your work?', she offered a more direct interpretation, saying that 'they exist in nature, they exist in life'.[3] While she usually avoided didactic explanations of her art, a sense of the organic runs throughout much of her work, particularly in the biomorphic shapes that started appearing in the early 1930s, through to the 1940s pictures of barrage balloons (fig.59), with similar floating forms mutating and reappearing in her works from the late 1940s onwards, such as *Eight Curved Forms and Two Circles* (1946; fig.3) and the black and white wooden relief *Lines in Space No.51* (1965; fig.4).

It also informs her textile designs, which started in 1945 and would become an extraordinary (and commercially popular) output that is only now being fully appreciated. As Helen Janecek writes, in both 1959 and 1962 she had seven designs in production with Heal's, placing her among their top five designers during the period. These designs varied enormously in style, ranging from graphic lines and geometric shapes to more rounded, undulating forms. Some would be directly inspired by specific images, such as the depiction of an atom seen in a book about the microscope that had belonged to her grandfather, which would become her textile *Parade* (1957).

Vézelay scrutinised the world with a forensic curiosity, never forgetting a lifetime of visual cues that would shape her vision: the silhouette of Christmas presents seen in the early morning from her bed as a young child; the flash of a turning fish in a chalk stream; the folds of cloth of a 15th-century buddha sculpture; the Cirque Medrano trapeze artists; pressed seaweed; the stark outline of a Viking helmet; the shadows cast on a Somerset country walk.

In later years she would find renewed inspiration in her overgrown south-London garden. Based on a design that she had created several decades earlier, and with echoes of the shapes of her 1930s plaster sculptures, this garden was, one could argue, the largest artwork she ever made. Everything that Vézelay applied herself to was done with remarkable rigour, perseverance and passion. This would explain why, as Vézelay's niece Sally Jarman remembered, 'like Turner, whom she much admired, she came to think of her works as her own children and became reluctant to part with them at any price', preferring to preserve her 'dignified, unworldly integrity'.

Despite the struggles that she encountered in her life, most notably the slow acceptance by her country of birth to fully recognise her talents, Vézelay loved what she did and maintained a strong faith in her art to the end. And what is apparent when we experience her art now is that, underlying all of it, is a great sense of joy in what she created. Hers are images that celebrate the labyrinthine twists and turns of a life positively lived, and it is this joy that is her great legacy.

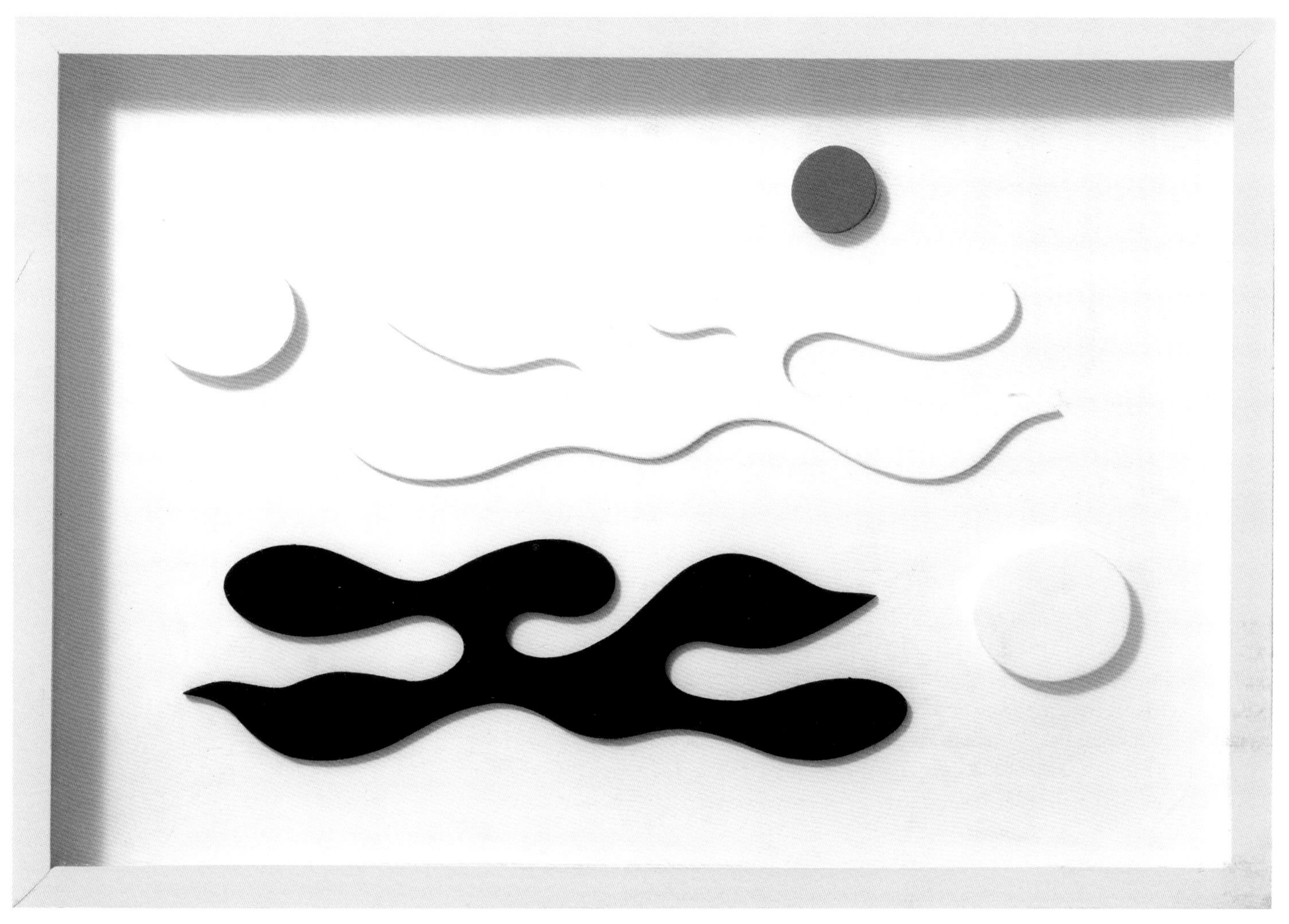

4
Paule Vézelay, *Lines in Space No.51*, 1965,
mixed media construction, 39.5 × 57.5 × 5.5 cm,
Estate of Paule Vézelay

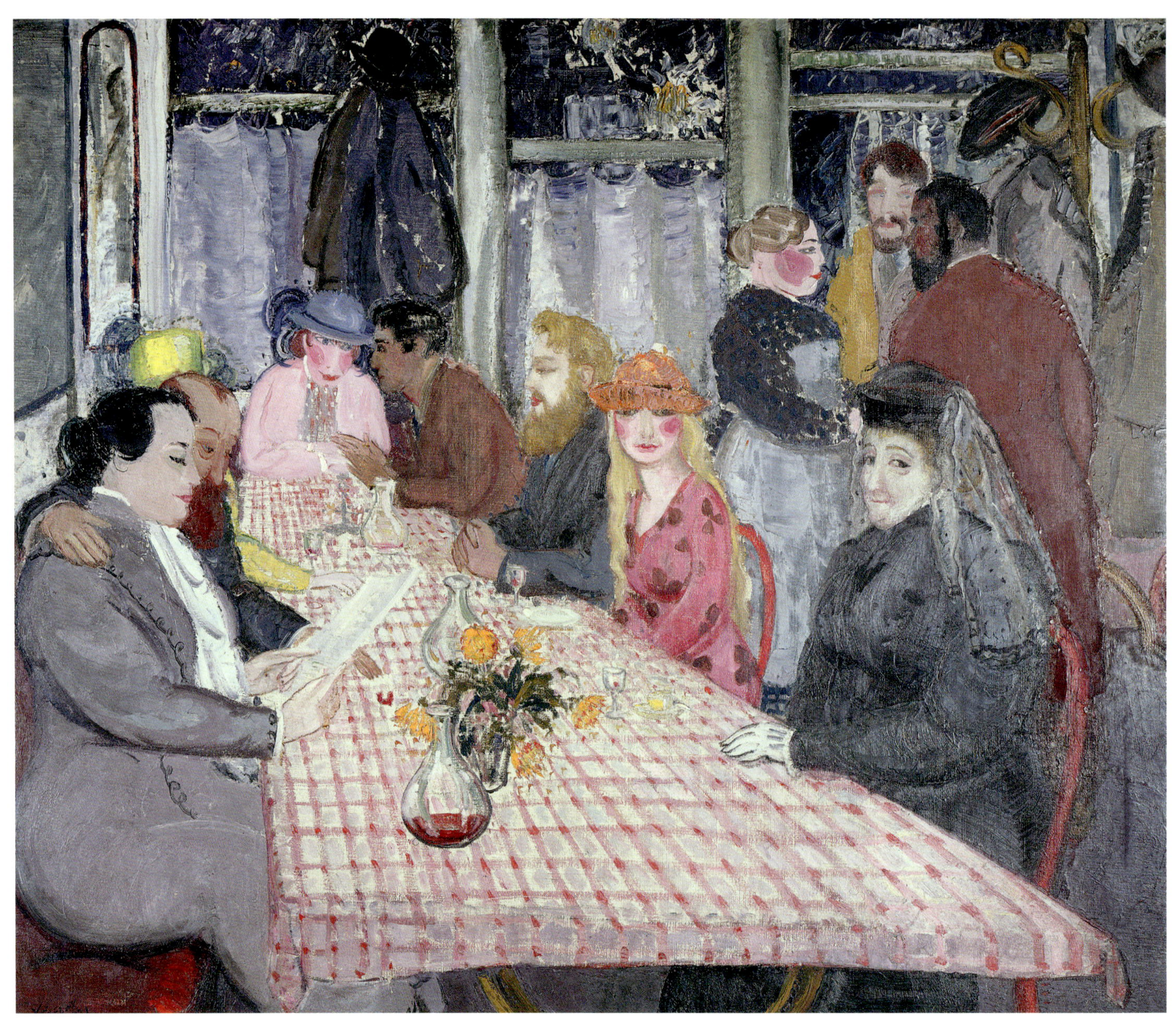

5
Marjorie Watson-Williams / Paule Vézelay,
In a Paris Restaurant, 1921, oil on canvas,
81.3 × 100.5 cm, private collection

Simon Grant

Paule Vézelay: The Making of an International Artist

> *The best of the women painters, whose heart stirs with a novelty and freshness superior to most of the halfmen.*[1]

Paule Vézelay (born Marjorie Watson-Williams) knew from early on in her career that it was in France, not England, that she could make it as an artist. Here lived the artists that she had admired since childhood, some of whom, such as Henri Matisse and Juan Gris, were still alive. She would spend her most radical years in Paris, while navigating her way through the art world with the help of her enterprising gallerists and a wide circle of friends, among them many like-minded women artists whom she met there. She would later remember with pride how she knew 'seventeen different nationalities' in Paris, and over time she would be acknowledged by many of them as a ground-breaking international artist.[2]

Vézelay began her art journey in her hometown of Bristol. After three years at art school there, she moved to London in 1912, where she continued her training at the London School of Art, until the outbreak of the First World War. Successful work as an illustrator followed, done alongside her painting, both of which reflected her fascination with observing people. However, war over-shadowed everything, and she spent many days with her mother, Margaret, at a Red Cross centre, where one of her jobs was moulding papier mâché casts for wounded soldiers, giving her an early sense for sculptural form. Her time during the war was also taken up with an intense relationship with one of the Belgian refugees, the painter Léon de Smet (1881–1966), whose uplifting palette would influence Vézelay's own.

Vézelay's wish to distance herself from de Smet's claustrophobic advances would prompt her first visit to Paris in 1920. Within a few months she was exhibiting at the Galerie des Feuillets d'Art (a new venue where Matisse and Picasso would show the following year), with a subsequent review in the literary newspaper *Comœdia* favourably comparing her pictures, including *Bristol Hippodrome* (1918–19; fig.6), to Pierre Bonnard. Encouraged by this, she would write poetically about Paris, with 'her beautiful silver river, a ribbon of light and life, the ghosts which haunt her old slanting houses, the fountains which shoot up skywards towards the blue sky'.[3] These evocative descriptions would anticipate the floating verticals, horizontals and serpentine lines in her future abstract works.

The colour and rhythm of the city soon led to more ambitious narrative compositions, including *In a Paris Restaurant* (1921; fig.5), in which the intimate human drama of a meal is played out in a beautifully observed choreography

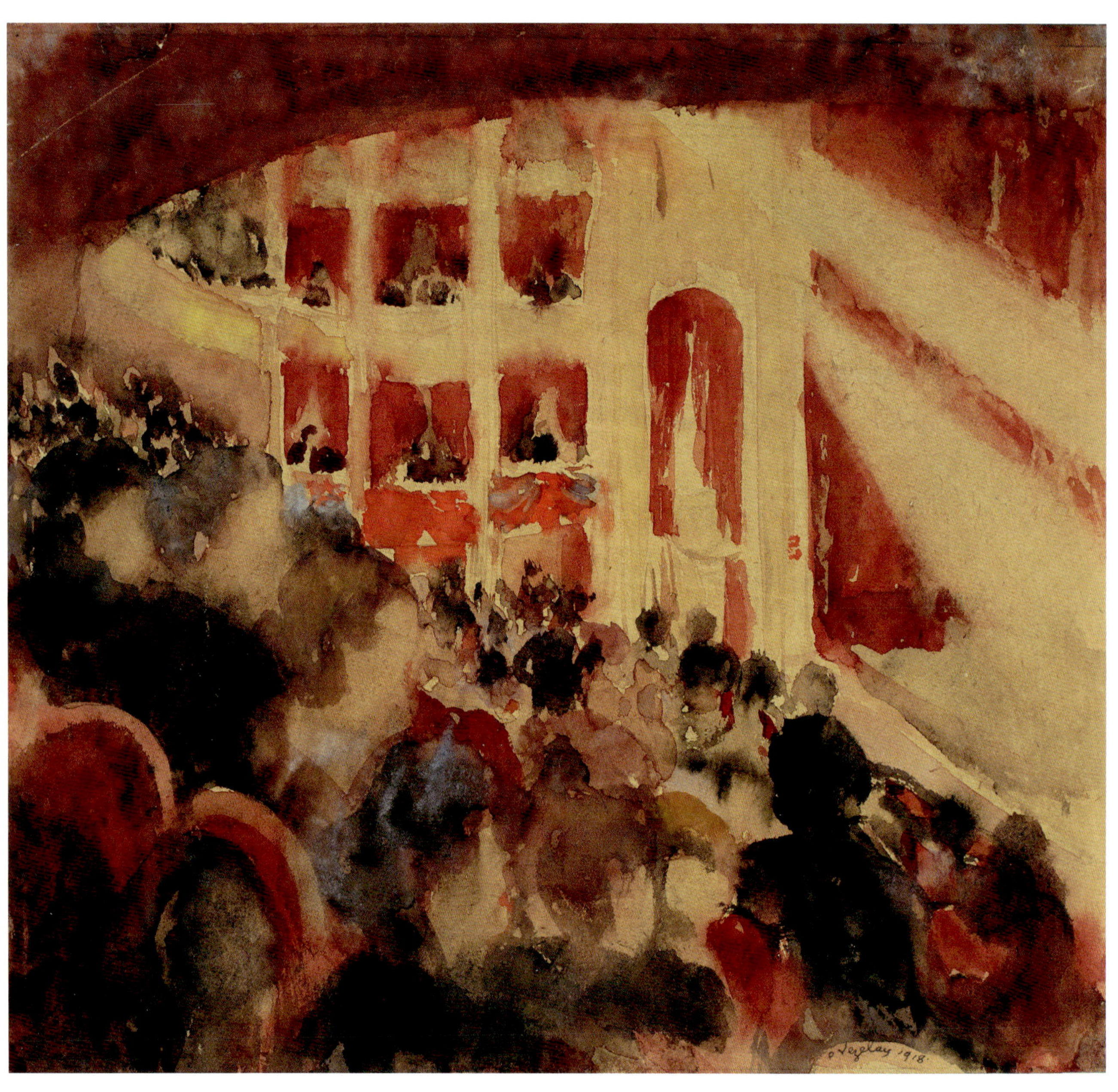

6
Marjorie Watson-Williams / Paule Vézelay,
Bristol Hippodrome, c.1918–19, watercolour,
28 × 30 cm, University of Bristol Theatre Collection

of pinks, purples and greys. Vézelay was also drawn to the Cirque Medrano, a venue that had inspired artists as various as Picasso, Modigliani, Toyen and Miró. Its key attraction was the Fratellini brothers, whose flamboyant escapades inspired some of Vézelay's paintings, such as *Three Clowns at Medrano* (c.1923, now lost; fig.7). Paul, François and Albert Fratellini were so popular that they regularly opened their dressing room to fans, including Vézelay, who would portray Paul, post-performance, in a striking print.

7
Three Clowns at Medrano (c.1923) by Marjorie Watson-Williams / Paule Vézelay, photograph by Paule Vézelay, Tate Archive

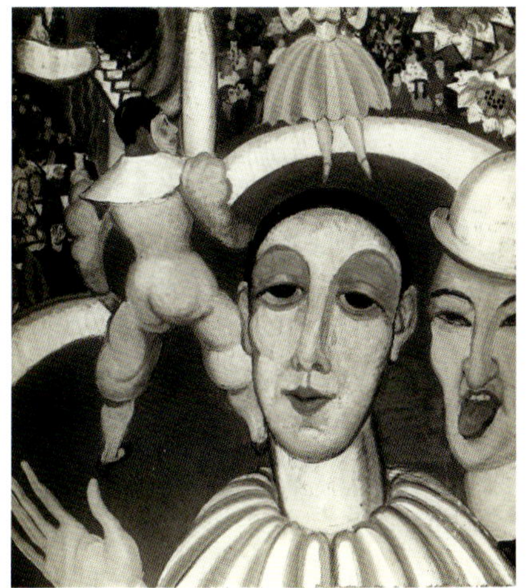

Vézelay was quick to develop friendships in Paris. Through the writer John Galsworthy she connected with the pioneering dancer Margaret Morris, who was living with the Scottish Colourist J.D. Fergusson. Vézelay was drawn to their vigorous ideas and their fascination with the power of rhythm to elevate life. Morris regarded dance as highly liberating, as 'a living art . . . capable of expressing the ideas and emotions of the 20th century',[4] while Fergusson followed Henri Bergson's idea of *élan vital* (vital life force), which he channelled into paintings and sculptures of athletic women.

In the summer of 1923 Vézelay joined the couple at Morris's dance school at the Cap d'Antibes on the French Riviera. Here, she spent the hot days swimming, as well as watching Loïs Hutton, Hélène Vanel and other barefoot dancers led by Morris underneath the shadows of the palm trees, and meeting new people, including Fergusson's old friend Pablo Picasso. Her subsequent pictures, including *The Bathers* (1923; fig.25), would reflect the collective energy of that summer.

Vézelay exhibited *The Bathers* alongside Parisian café and circus pictures in her first solo exhibition at the Galerie Louis Manteau, Brussels, in 1924, facilitated by de Smet. Several of the pictures would go on to be shown at the Château des Enfants, a vast villa in Cap d'Antibes owned by Morris and Fergusson's generous, spirited friend George Davison, a photographer and former managing director of Kodak UK. Thanks to Davison, the exhibition attracted the notice of a *Daily Mail* correspondent, who described how Vézelay had 'seized with adroit artistry the difference between the vivid, clear-cut, all enveloping sunlight of the Riviera, and the softer, greyer, more restful atmosphere of England'.[5]

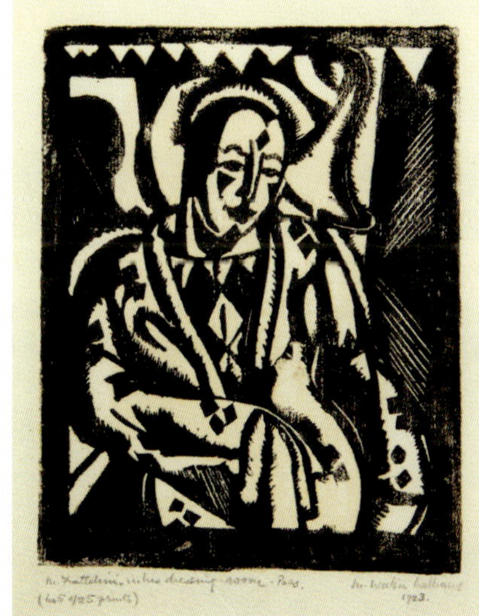

8
Marjorie Watson-Williams / Paule Vézelay, *Mr. Fratellini in his Dressing Room*, 1923, woodcut, 18.5 × 15.5 cm, Royal West of England Academy, Bristol

Vézelay moved more permanently to Paris in 1926, finding a well lit studio on the fourth floor on Rue de la Grande Chaumière in Montparnasse, from where she would reflect her feelings of being more settled to a friend, writing: 'I am very much alive, full of happiness in my work and friends.'[6] A few months later she cemented her new life by changing her name to Paule Vézelay, the surname inspired by the 12th-century Romanesque Vézelay Abbey in Burgundy. The first name – a recognised French girl's name – was chosen, as she wrote to fellow artist Ithell Colquhoun, to avoid 'this question of sex [being] dragged into discussions about my work'. Yet she also insisted that she be still regarded as an English artist.[7]

Her new name featured in the publicity for her exhibition at the Galerie Alice Manteau in Paris in 1928, in which visitors could see her subtle shift from illustrative figuration towards a more tubular, blocky style, in part inspired, as *The Chicago Tribune* critic noted, by Juan Gris, whom Vézelay had interviewed the previous year. After praising Vézelay's work for its 'rare sense of colour and line', the critic then gave readers an unexpected interpretation of her circus paintings, writing how Vézelay had been kidnapped while a child in England by gypsies who 'taught her to walk the tight rope and stand on the backs of galloping horses'.[8] Whether this fanciful story came from Vézelay or was journalistic licence remains unclear.

Everything would suddenly change at a party in spring 1929, when the German writer and art critic Carl Einstein introduced Vézelay to André Masson. There was an immediate attraction, and this began what would be the most intense relationship of Vézelay's life. At first, she was unaware that Masson was 'a 50% war-wounded nervous case' due to his experience in the First World War, when he was left injured and hallucinating in no man's land.[9] Vézelay would have empathised with Masson's experience. Both her younger brothers had served on the Western Front, with Eric at Ypres and brother Guthrie (aged only 17) at Marne. Guthrie was blown up by a mine and suffered severe shell shock. Masson's own post-traumatic mood swings and physically violent behaviour towards Vézelay were exacerbated by the side effects of the anti-epilepsy barbiturate Luminal. Outwardly, Vézelay masked her anxieties, yet, as she wrote in a note to Gertrude Stein, she struggled with her 'double life', as both partner and artist.[10] As Sarah Wilson's writes, the effect on both the style and content of her painting was marked.

After her final break with Masson in 1932, her painting style loosened, and a more confident picture composition emerged. It was as if her line, previously bound and tethered, had become unleashed. This period also signalled her return to exploring a more explicit sense of movement in space, epitomised by works such as *Dancing Forms* (1933; fig.28) and *Personnage Tenant une Fleur* (1933). The latter was painted in Spain and was partly inspired by time spent with Joan Miró and his wife, Pilar, in Barcelona in May 1932, during which they saw performances of Léonide Massine's ballets *Les Présages* (with sets designed by Masson) and *Jeux d'enfants* (with set designs by Miró).

Vézelay's art was by this time reflecting shifts in the European avant-garde, where the boundaries between abstraction and Surrealism were beginning to blur. Some of these tendencies would be on display in the exhibitions staged by Abstraction-Création, an artist-led association showcasing new abstract art by artists from as far afield as Japan and Australia, with whom several of Vézelay's friends, including Marlow Moss and Jeanne Kosnick-Kloss, would also exhibit. In the third Abstraction-Création exhibition, in December 1933, Vézelay premiered her new painting *Strange Landscape* (1933; fig.12), not a landscape at all, but a vibrant combination of curved conical forms and abstracted shapes. It was the result of Vézelay's intensive exploration of a visual language with, as she put it, 'colours and forms more pleasing than can easily be found in actuality or seen by [the] unaided imagination'.[11] *Strange Landscape* exemplified the emergence of this biomorphic art (a term coined by the art critic Geoffrey Grigson after visiting the 1934 Abstraction-Création exhibition), which was also apparent in the art of fellow exhibitors, including Jean Arp, Barbara Hepworth, J.W. Power and Tarō Okamoto. As Grigson explained, they were exploring the balance 'between idea and emotion, between matter and mind, matter and life.'[12]

Less than two months later, *Strange Landscape* would be shown again, this time as one of the main pictures in Vézelay's first exhibition with the influential Galerie Jeanne Bucher in 1934. Bucher had been following Vézelay's development since visiting her studio in 1927, becoming her greatest champion as well as a firm friend, and was delighted by her new stylistic direction. Keen to state her art-world credentials, Vézelay ensured that the catalogue listed works already owned by key international art figures, including Christian

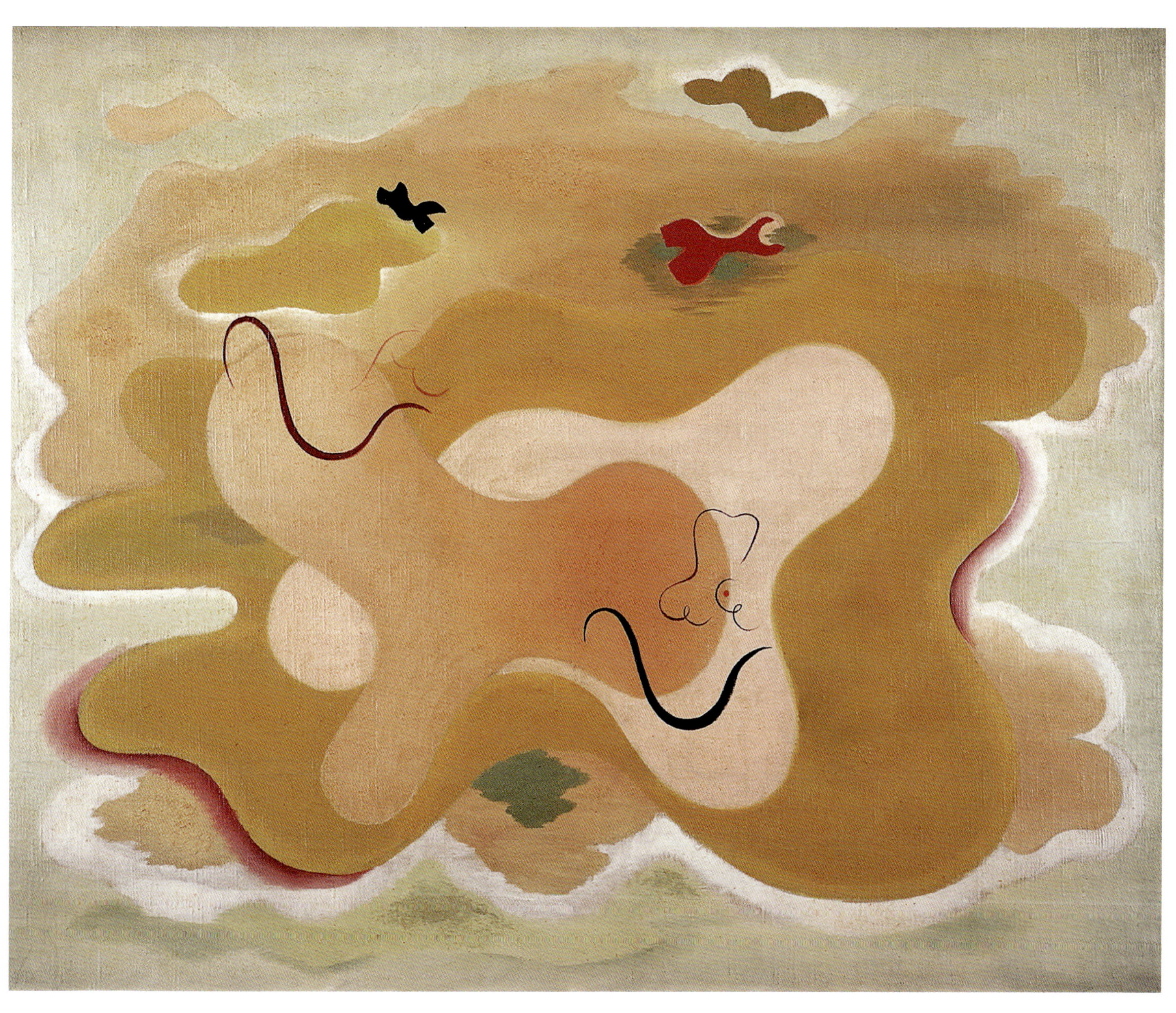

9
Paule Vézelay, *The Sunbathers*, 1929, oil on canvas, 73 × 93 cm, private collection

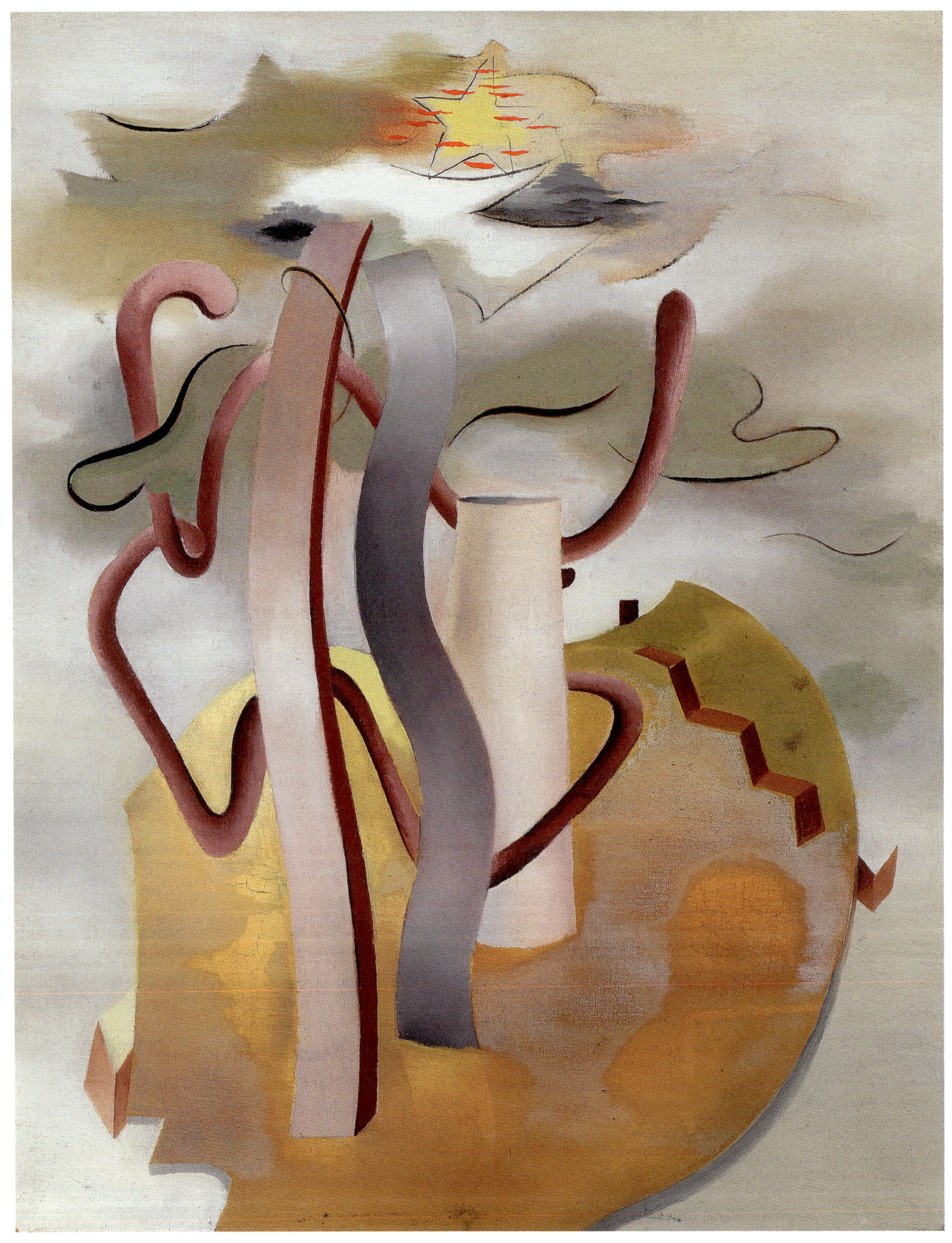

10
Paule Vézelay, *Composition Objects and Sun*, 1930, oil on canvas, 51.5 × 41 cm, private collection

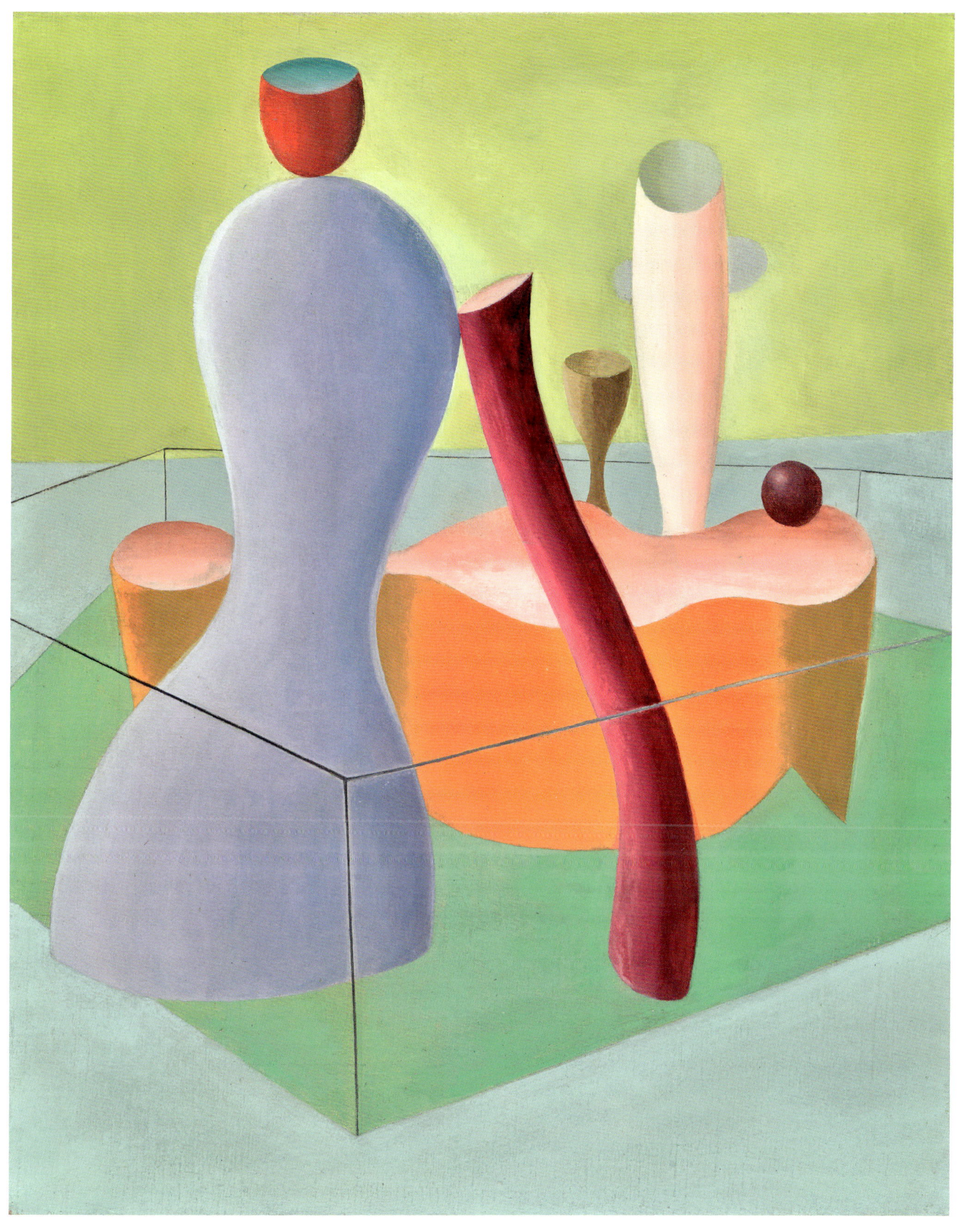

11
Paule Vézelay, *Composition*, 1934, oil on canvas, 72 × 34 cm,
Collection Musée Zervos, Vézelay – Conseil départemental de l'Yonne

12
Paule Vézelay, *Strange Landscape*, 1933, oil on canvas, 65 × 80.9 cm, Tate

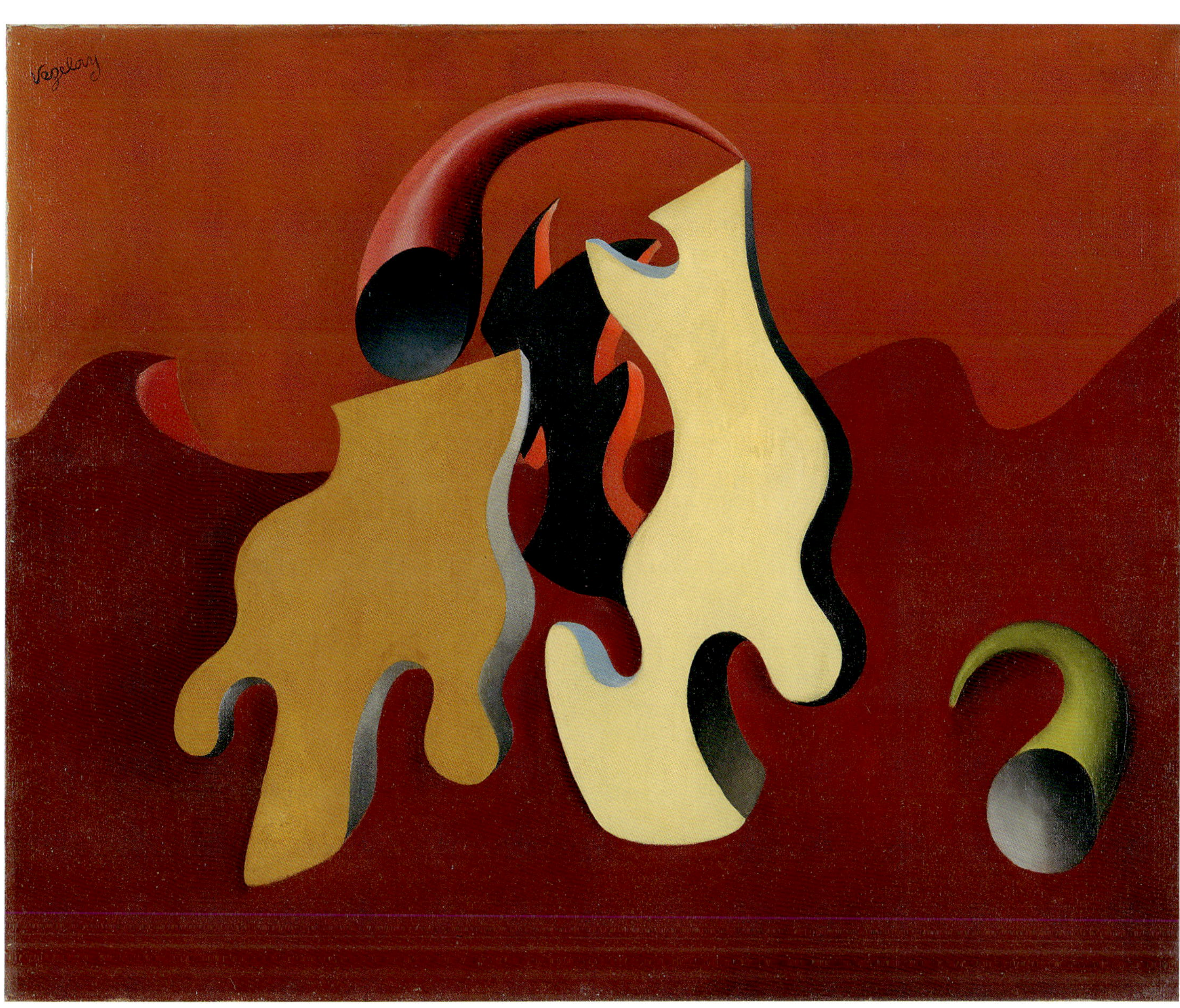

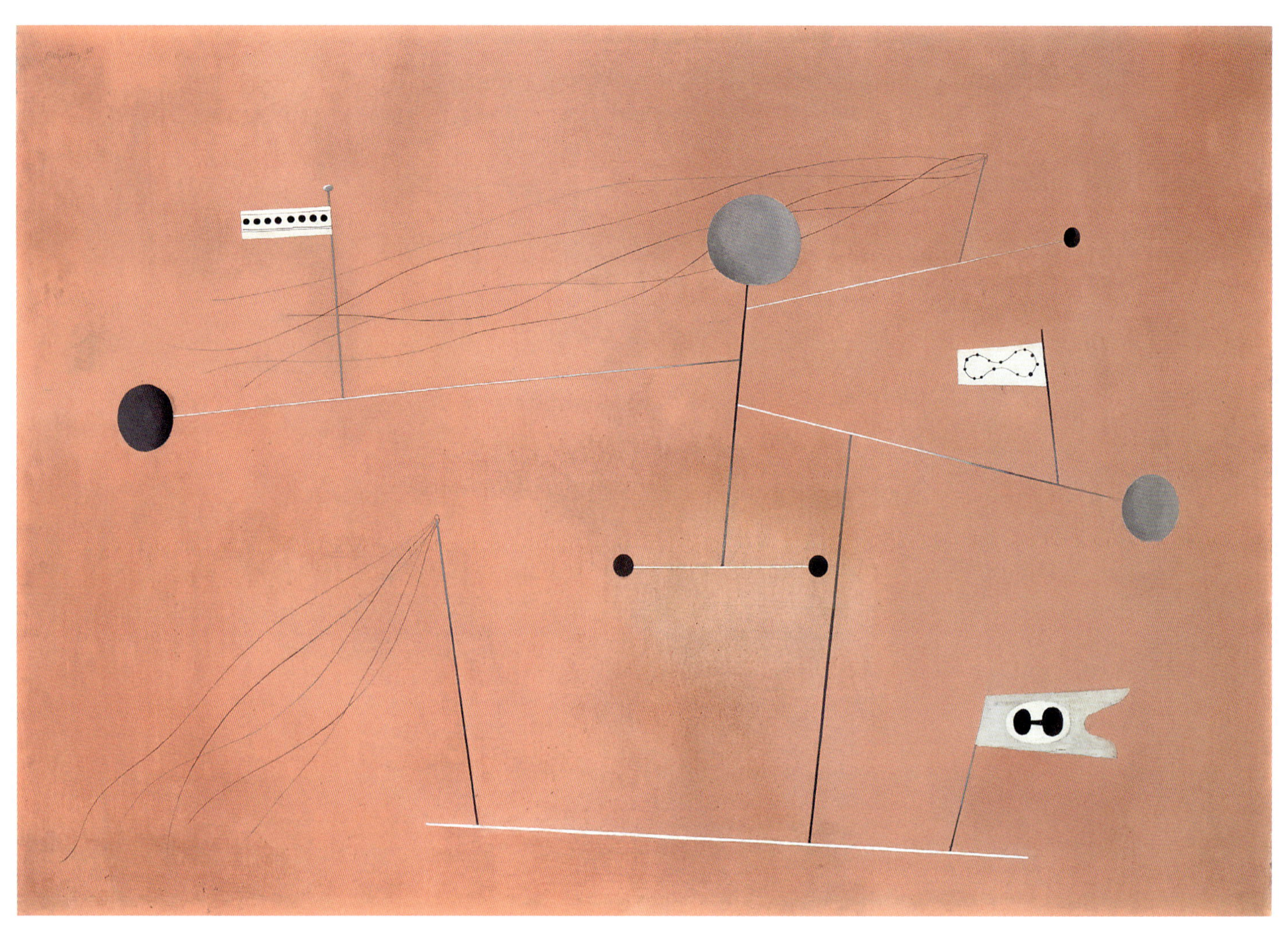

13
Paule Vézelay, *Construction. Grey Lines on Pink Ground*, 1938, oil on canvas, 81.3 × 115.9 cm, Tate

Zervos, a collector and the editor of *Cahiers d'Art*, and Marguerite Duthuit, the daughter of Matisse and one of her close friends in Paris. Vézelay and Duthuit would later co-host a French fashion show of Duthuit's designs at Vézelay's parents' house in Bristol.

Around this time Vézelay met Sophie Taeuber-Arp and her husband, Jean Arp. After Masson, these would be the most important friends she would have in France. In Taeuber-Arp Vézelay found a strong, quietly driven woman with 'perfect equilibrium', whose thoughtful approach to line and form, fed by her early passion for dance, firmly resonated with Vézelay's own art-making.[13] Beyond their conversations around art and friendship, often at the Arps' house in Meudon in the Paris suburbs, Vézelay and Taeuber-Arp also discussed the difficulties of being a female artist at that time. In one letter Taeuber-Arp complained about men, who 'will never understand that you can not [sic] do your own work with the left hand, while the right one is in the kitchen, the ears at the telephone and the feet are doing errands'.[14]

While Taeuber-Arp's squares, rectangles, circles and straight lines could look markedly different to Vézelay's more serpentine lines, there were moments of synergy, most notably in Vézelay's *Construction. Grey Lines on Pink Ground* (1938; fig.13), which bears similarities to Taeuber-Arp's *Équilibre* series begun in 1931. It is possible that Vézelay's more fluid line would, in part, influence Taeuber-Arp's own series *Line Movements* (1939–41), drawings of snake-like forms that flow, entangle, merge and move apart. In turn, Vézelay was drawn to Arp's fluid 'Concretion' sculptures, such as *Sculpture to Be Lost in the Forest* (fig.15), a 1932 work with moveable parts that Arp gave to Vézelay and would inspire the latter's own move into sculpture from 1935. Her white plasters, such as *Dish and Little Boat* (1935–6), also featured detachable pieces, an idea extended in her piece *Garden* (1935; fig.16), with its arrangement of sand, shells, sea urchins and starfishes found on French beaches.

It is clear that all three artists had a deep connection to the natural world, yet they were reluctant to articulate this directly. Arp would write, though, about how Taeuber-Arp 'radiated with happiness' in nature, often talking to the flowers and the stars.[15] From 1936 her works featured increasingly organic forms, as seen in the wooden relief series *Shell and Flower* (1938). Arp, who had grown up near the Black Forest and who for many years had been attracted to the non-rational and poetic potential of nature, regarded his 'Concretions' as signifying natural processes – 'the curdling of the earth and the heavenly bodies . . . the mass of the stone, the plant, the animal, the man.'[16]

Vézelay insisted that her abstract works were pure imaginary inventions, yet her art repeatedly suggested otherwise. Like many other artists who trod a biomorphic path, the organic-looking forms in her paintings and sculptures often had biological or zoological origins or influences. First appearing in the 1930s, these elements would feature in many different subtle developments in subsequent paintings, sculptures and textiles. They would be most explicit in some of her pictures done after the Second World War, as in the stridently coloured verticals in *Growing Forms* (1946; fig.17) and the dark, looming, leaf-like shapes in *Contact – Four Grey Forms* (1973; fig.18). Sometimes her organic narrative could almost appear diaristic, as in the fishing line, flies, pebbles and feathers that constitute the composition of *Objects in Three Dimensions* (1935; fig.19), no doubt inspired by the regular trout fishing trips outside Paris that she took on rare days off from the studio.

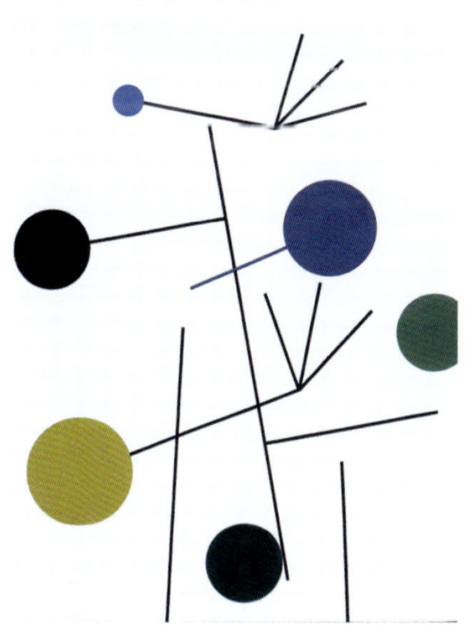

14
Sophie Taeuber-Arp, *Équilibre*, 1934, oil on canvas, 99.8 × 73.3 cm, Kunstmuseum Basel

The white plaster sculptures of the curving forms of cones and cut ovals that debuted in Vézelay's second exhibition with Jeanne Bucher in 1937 also paid a partial debt to natural forms. Exhibited alongside these for the first time was her *Lines in Space* series. Announced as 'three-dimensional research', they consisted of cotton threads or thin pieces of wire pulled across the picture frame – sometimes interlocking – and set against a (predominantly) white background. Vézelay would regard these as among her most advanced creations. Describing them as pictures with 'living lines', which she believed went beyond the rational methods of the artist, she said that the process of making these pictures was 'in some degree controlled by a power far greater than any I could claim as my own.'[17] Vézelay was not alone in this type of thinking. Among her friends, Kandinsky had a long-held interest in theosophy, mysticism and spirituality, while Arp would explore the synthesis of the cosmic and the organic in his art and poetry.

Both Kandinsky and Arp would be among the stellar list of artists who came to the opening night at the Bucher exhibition, a list that also included Mondrian, Giacometti, Taeuber-Arp, Maria Helena Vieira da Silva, Florence Henri and Wolfgang Paalen. Above all, this signified that Vézelay's years of toil in the heart of the European avant-garde had finally come to fruition. The German art critic Herta Wescher would seal the collective approval, describing her *Lines in Space* works as 'little authentic masterpieces'.[18]

Soon, the *Lines in Space* works would be in demand, and over the next two years they were shown in several important group exhibitions, including the *Internationale de l'art non-figuratif*, at the Gemeentemuseum, Amsterdam (on Kandinsky's recommendation); *L'art concret* at Galleria Il Milione, Milan, where Vézelay exhibited alongside friends, including Taeuber-Arp and Kandinsky; and *Réalités nouvelles* at the Galerie Charpentier, Paris, the largest abstract art exhibition of its time.

Yet, just as her status as an international artist was assured, events beyond her control changed everything. Vézelay had been well aware of the political situation in Germany, with Taeuber-Arp sharing increasingly worrying news from Swiss family and friends in her letters to her. This was not a distant clamour. Kandinsky and Otto Freundlich, both of whom exhibited at Bucher's gallery, had been labelled as degenerate artists by the Nazis.

After a relatively peaceful holiday with the Arps and their extended family on the Brittany coast in the summer of 1939, Vézelay had little choice but to leave Paris, and one month after war was declared she travelled back to England. She returned to a country that was not only more conservative than the one she had lived in for nearly 20 years but that was also largely unaware of what she had achieved. Yet she would face this challenge with her characteristic resolve and would spend the following decades pushing and developing the boundaries of her art in new ways.

15
Jean Arp, *Sculpture to Be Lost in the Forest*, 1932 (cast c.1953–8), bronze, 9 × 22.2 × 15.4 cm, Tate

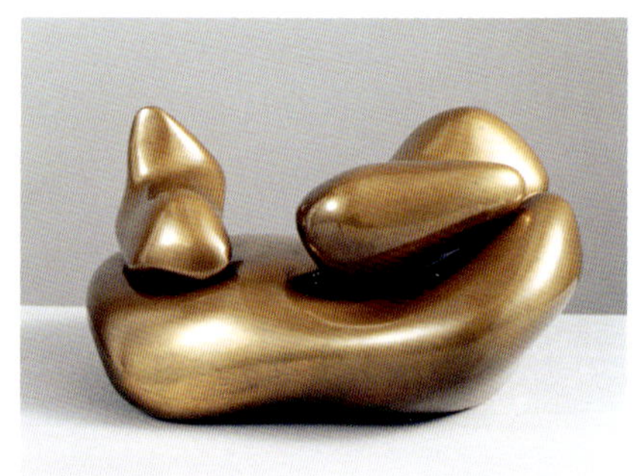

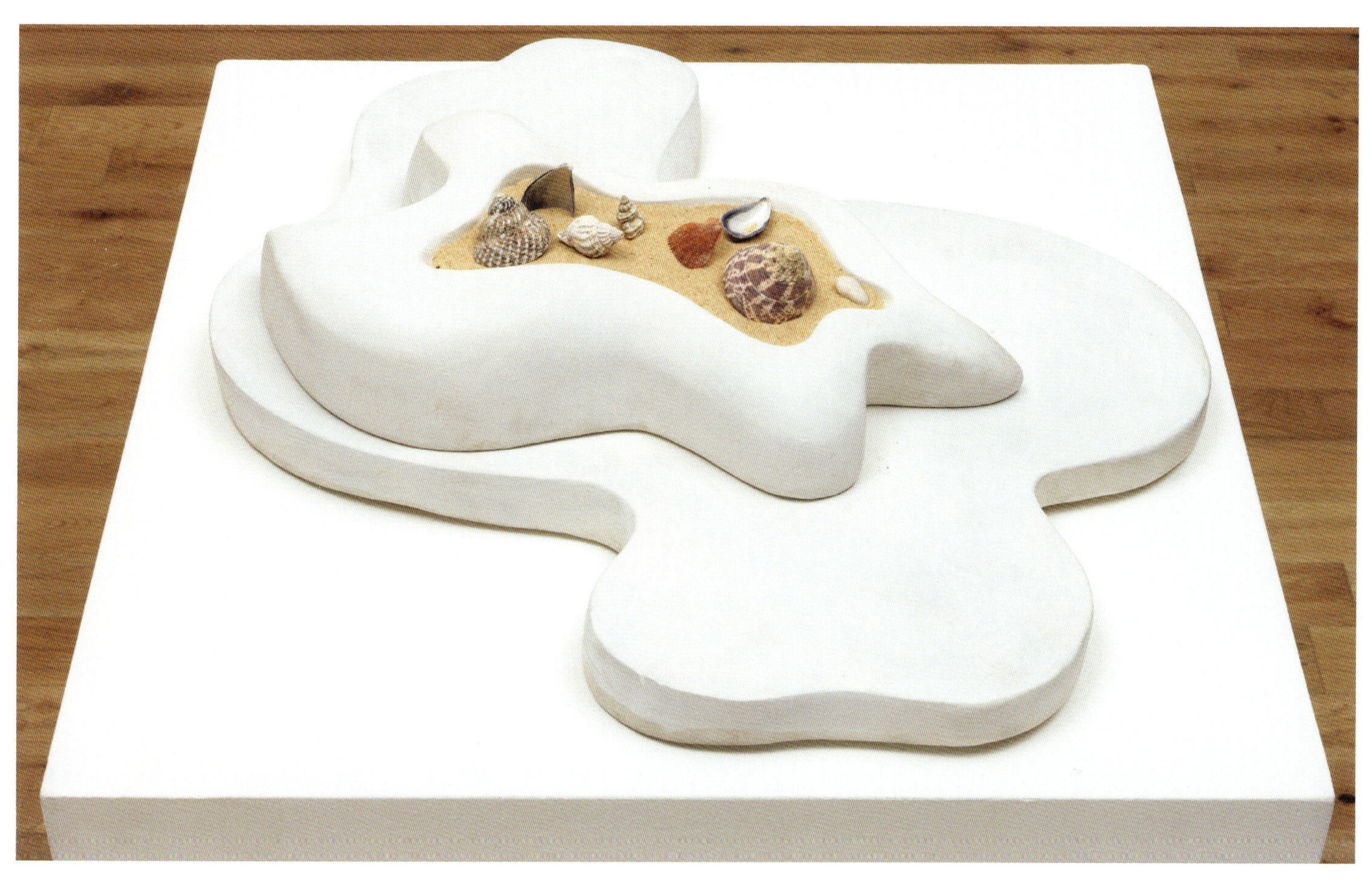

16
Paule Vézelay, *Garden*, 1935, plaster, paint, sand and shells, 7.5 × 59.5 × 42 cm, Tate

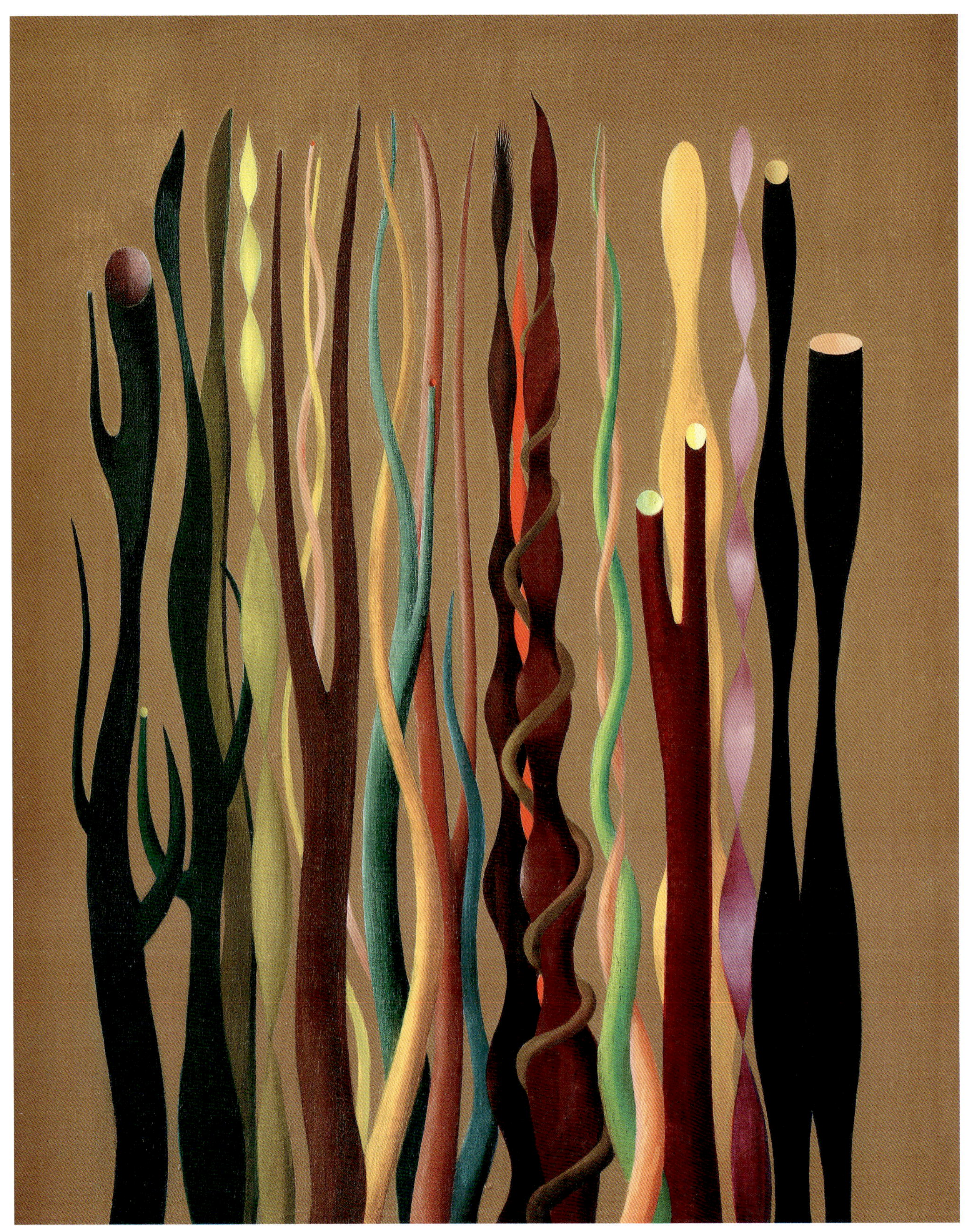

17
Paule Vézelay, *Growing Forms*, 1946, oil on canvas, 73 × 60 cm, private collection

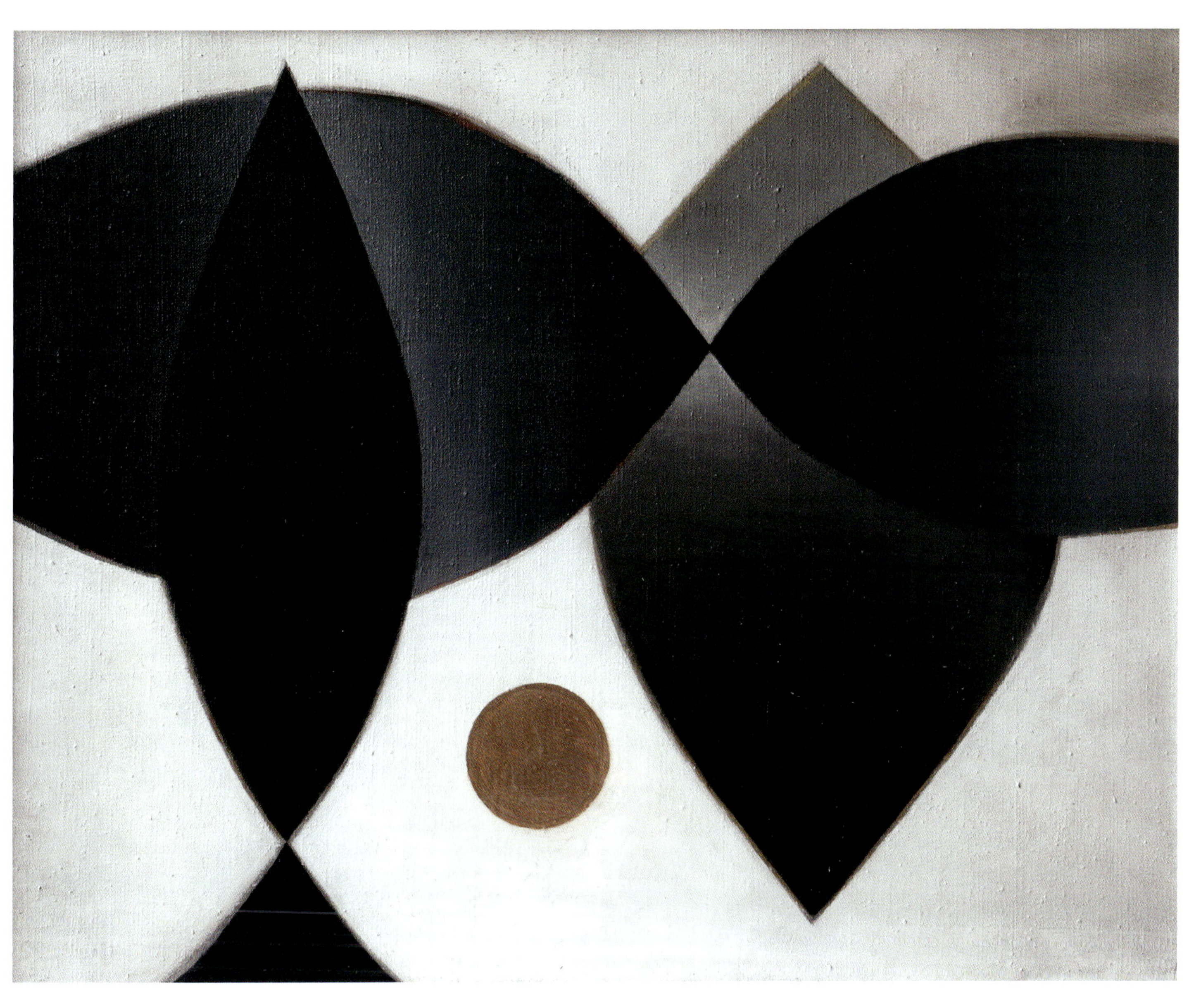

18
Paule Vézelay, *Contact – Four Grey Forms*, 1973,
oil on canvas, 74 × 92 cm, private collection

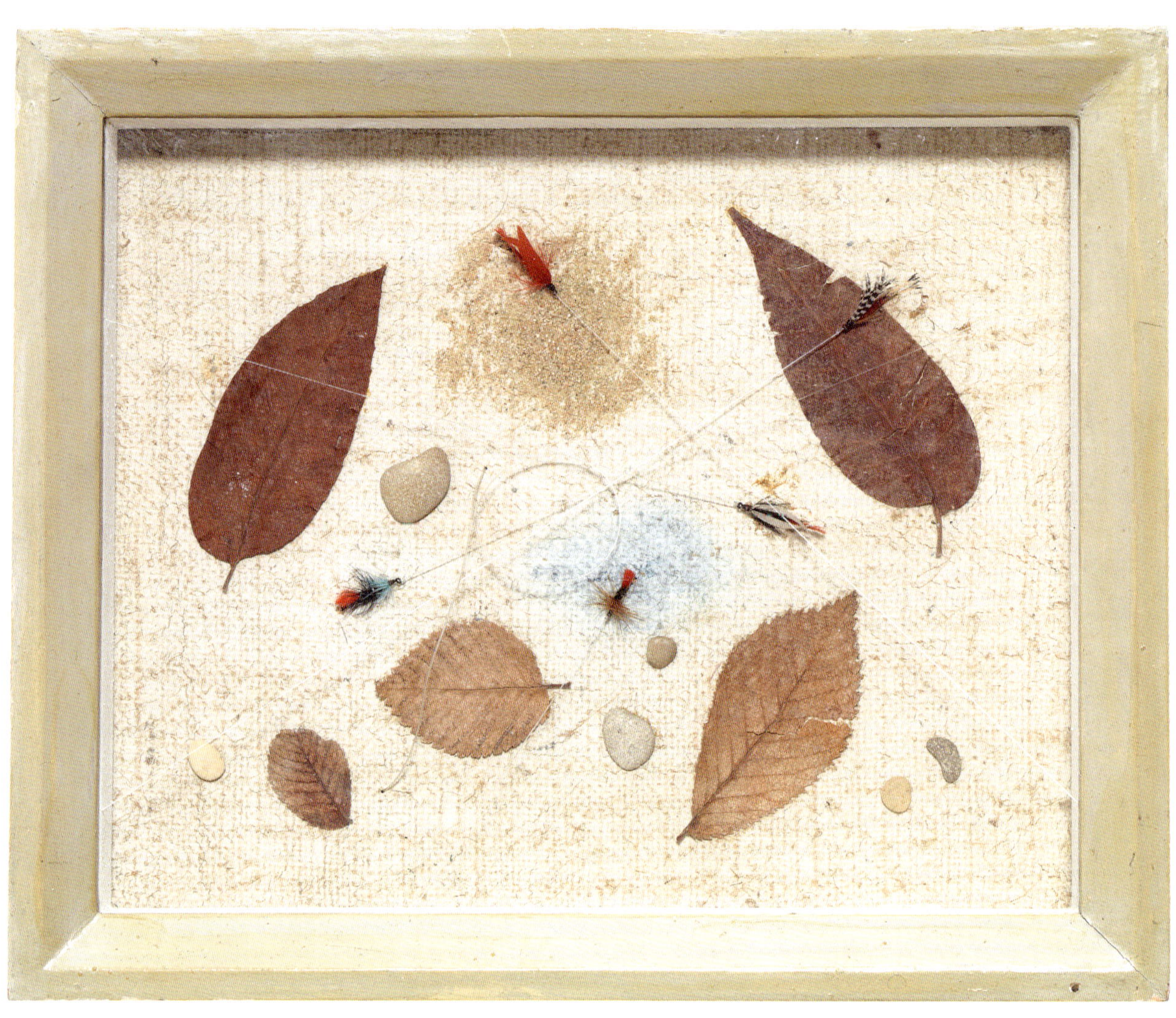

19
Paule Vézelay, *Object in Three Dimensions: Feather, Leaves, Fishing Flies*, 1935–6/1982, leaves, dry flies, fishing line, sand, pebbles and other materials on canvas, 22 × 27 × 5.5 cm, Tate

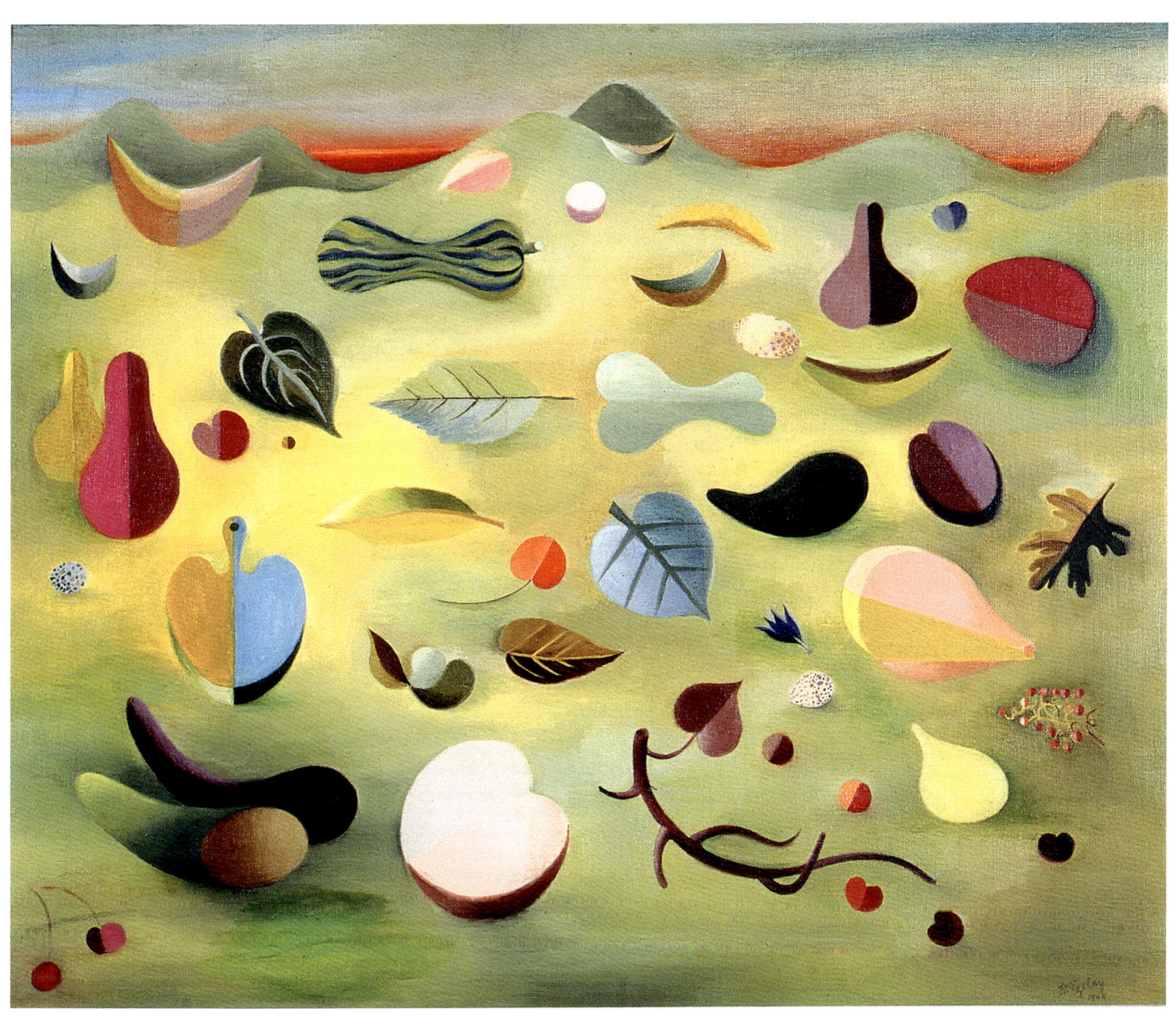

20
Paule Vézelay, *Paysage*, 1946, oil on canvas, 60 × 74 cm, private collection

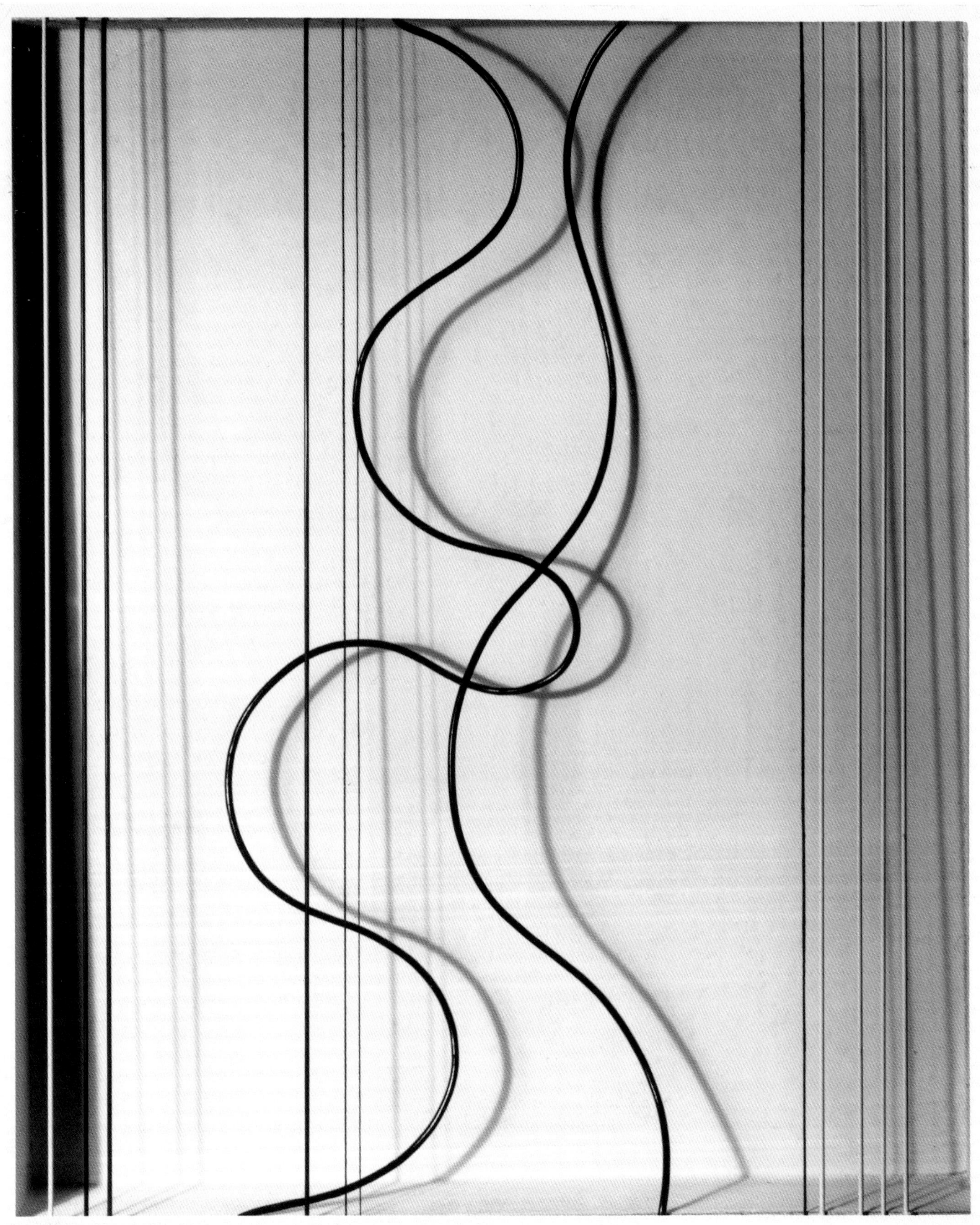

'And I Dance'

I stretched out ropes from spire to spire;
garlands from window to window;
golden chains from star to star, and I dance.[1]

Paule Vézelay recalled these melodic and magical words from Arthur Rimbaud's poem *Phrases* (1886) in the catalogue for an exhibition in 1942 of her series *Lines in Space*. Later, she considered the series the culmination of a life's work and her most significant contribution to abstract art, continually seeking out new ways with which to bring to life what she called her 'living lines'.

Rimbaud's garlands and golden constellations set the stage upon which to explore these 'living lines', which inhabited a multitude of forms and mediums throughout Vézelay's long career. Reviewing her Tate retrospective in 1983, Sarah Wilson also lingered on Rimbaud's words, declaring that Vézelay's 'whole adventure' can be found between the 'sublime liberty' and the 'delicate, boxed-in mystery' of her *Lines in Space*.[2] The 'adventure' of Vézelay's 'living lines' guides my own interest in the artist's work, explored by following a thread that runs throughout her interests in illustration, theatre, circus and dance, and that intertwines elements of Surrealism, abstraction and biomorphism, while also interweaving elements of her writing – spanning poetry, prose, educational guides, criticism and a film script.

Writing specifically about *Lines in Space*, Vézelay explained the importance of the line, which she considered to be the 'language of the artist since primitive man'.[3] Her ideas can be explored in greater detail in the educational text 'Basic Elements in the Science of Drawing and Composition', which she began in 1946 and continued revising until the 1970s.[4] Here, among words intended for students and amateurs, she establishes two fundamental lines – the straight line and the curved line – which form the basis of her vocabulary. Writing about her work for the Tate Gallery, London, in 1964, these lines assume an even greater reverence: 'when lines are drawn by a skilled and sensitive artist they are sometimes imbued with an almost celestial quality which miraculously imbues them with "Life" . . . feeling that these lines did indeed come from my hand and my Spirit . . . that they were inevitable.'[5]

This divine destiny which Vézelay bestows upon the simple line also reveals the delicate balancing act which lies at the heart of her work: ' . . . the artist must find the point of balance which lies between the parallel lines of pure reason, and desire; firmly balanced there he is able to unite these parallel lines with nothing more tangible than his mystic power of imagination, and his comprehending submission to the divine laws of balance.'[6] This much-

21
Paule Vézelay, *Straight and Curved Lines in Space and Thin Shadows: Construction No.16*, 1952, photograph by Paule Vézelay, Tate Archive

sought-for equilibrium appears in a revised, English version of *Imagination, mathématiques et équilibre* (Imagination, Mathematics and Balance), originally written by Vézelay to accompany an exhibition at Galerie Colette Allendy, Paris, in 1947. The later version revisits the idea of objectivity and reason in relation to the imagination, suggesting that the slow and sometimes painful process of creating 'what is invisible and intangible' and expressing 'emotions, not scenes' can create works that bring us an 'escape from reality' and 'entice us to wander in the world of magic that only imagination can sometimes create'. Yet, despite this beguiling call, artists must still find a way to confront and balance their 'spiritual or emotional' concerns and their 'entirely mathematical or geometrical' concerns.[7]

We could think of these dual concerns as parallel lines – the imagination a curved, meandering line and reason a logical, straight line – or metaphorically as Rimbaud's looping garlands and stretched ropes. Eager to understand the way in which these fundamental concerns might coexist, Vézelay provides us with many rich analogies to draw upon, often evoking music and poetry – subjects which reoccur throughout her writing – to conjure up a world in which the imagination and mathematics can live harmoniously, side by side.

Our own search begins by tracing a line from the very first 'dot that went for a walk', to quote the artist Paul Klee, whom Vézelay much admired. These first dots or footsteps can be found in the meandering line carved through the silken mudbanks of the River Avon in Bristol. In Vézelay's memoir she recalls how, as a child, she 'was free to wander along on the miles of Downs, that stretched far away over the top of the high cliffs which shelter part of the River Avon'. She remarks how this 'superbly beautiful Somerset landscape' had in part made her an artist, a belief she held dear throughout her life, maintaining that imagination first finds its feet by observing nature's organic rhythms.[8]

This first watery line was later replaced by the slow-flowing path of the River Seine, but before Paris was to leave its imprint, Vézelay undertook her formal artistic studies in England. She received her first lessons in nature's harmony at Bristol School of Art, drawing from life and studying Greek and Roman casts. This was followed by a short-lived stint at the Slade School of Fine Art, before studying drawing, painting and book illustration with the celebrated *Punch* draughtsman George Belcher at the London School of Art, with night classes in lithography at Chelsea Polytechnic sandwiched in between (1912–14). During this period Vézelay's focus remained on the human form, and she found success with her first published work, the illustrations to *A Diary of the Great Warr* by 'Saml. Pepys, Jnr' (1916; fig.22). This was followed by a series of popular illustrated essays for *Drawing and Design* (1917–22), for which she selected her own subjects, including 'The Theatre' and 'Music'. These graceful black and white illustrations pre-empted her preoccupation with bringing lines to life in the years that followed.

With her imagination now firmly stirred, Vézelay set her sights on Paris, the glittering centre of modern art. Visiting for the first time in 1920, she stayed at the Hôtel du Quai Voltaire, directly overlooking the winding Seine and the formal layout of the Jardin des Tuileries. Reflecting on her first impressions in 'Let Nothing be Lost Upon You' (her final contribution to *Drawing and Design*), she brings the river vividly to life: 'Below my open window lies the Seine, silver-grey, grey, green and silver; and the Louvre stretching itself above the moving water, a long grey mass ever waiting to thrill even the most bland of globe-

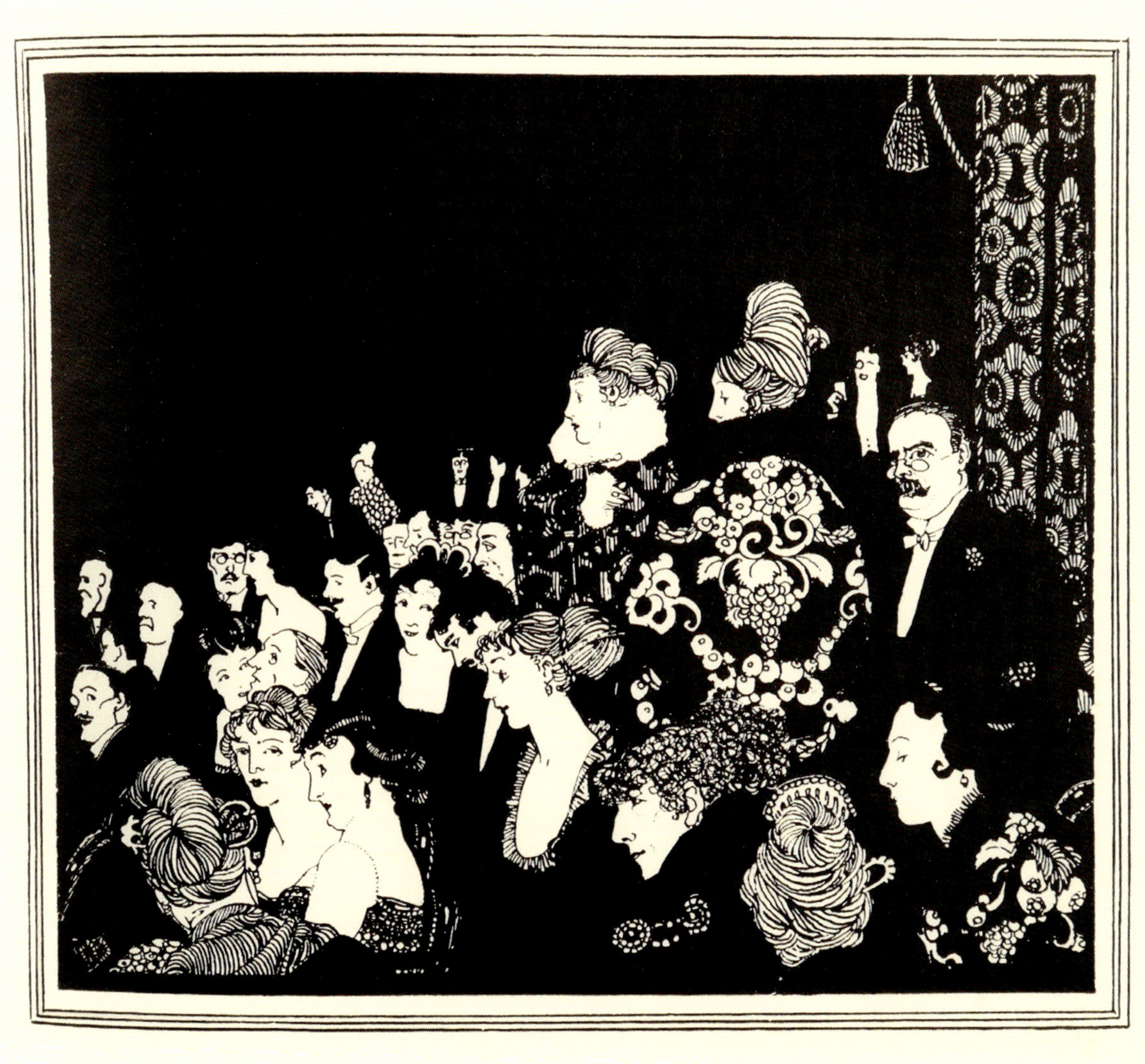

22
Marjorie Watson-Williams / Paule Vézelay,
At the Theatre, from *A Diary of the Great Warr*
by Saml. Pepys Jnr., illustrated by Marjorie
Watson-Williams / Paule Vézelay, 1919,
Estate of Paule Vézelay

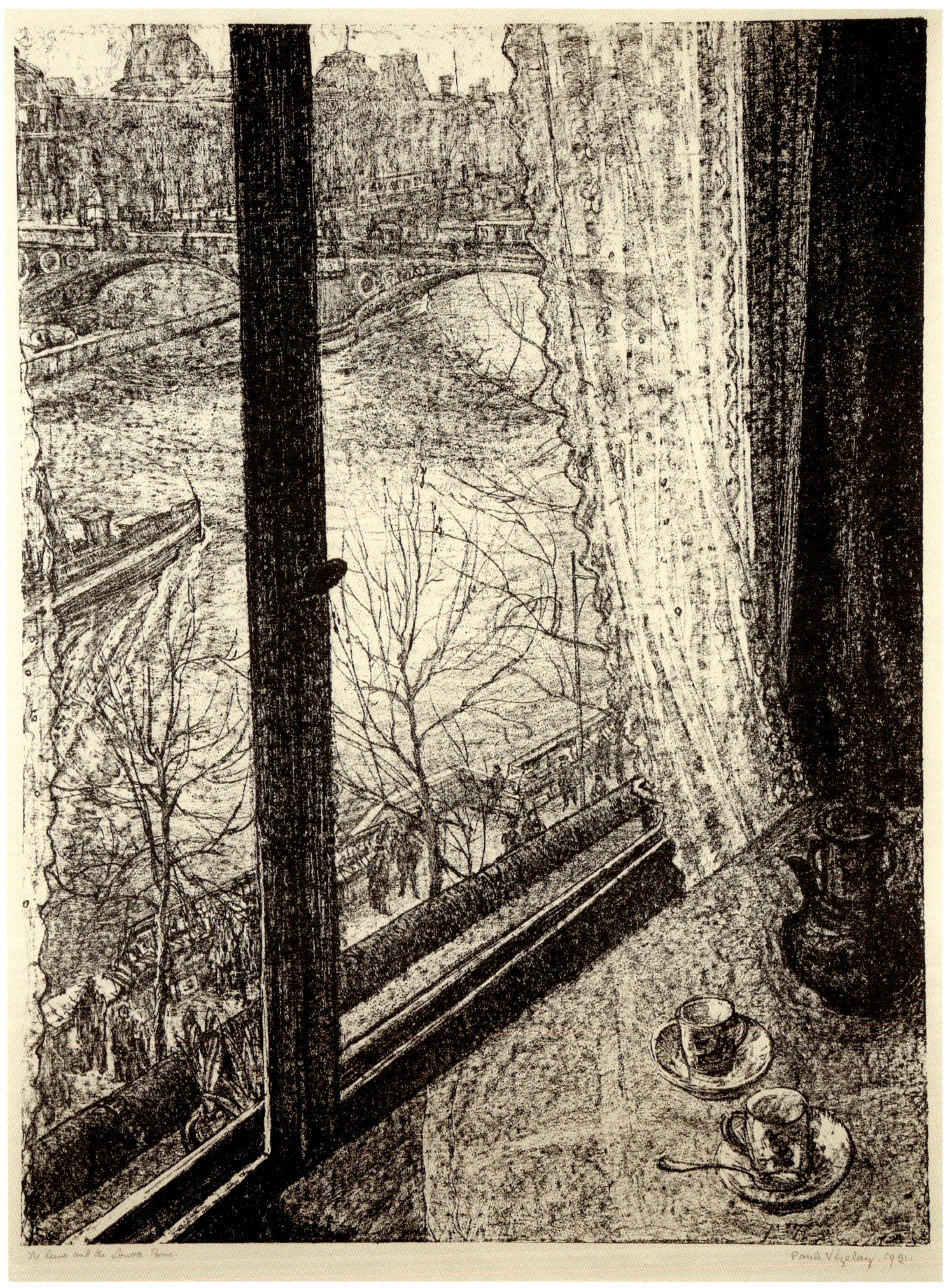

23
Marjorie Watson-Williams / Paule Vézelay,
Pont Neuf, 1921, lithograph, 44.2 × 57.7 cm,
Estate of Paule Vézelay

trotters . . . Paris, who draws to her side at one time or another every artist of the world.'[9]

Working amid the cafes, streets and theatres, she suggested that it was here in Paris that she first truly freed her imagination. Many early works feature views from the Hôtel du Quai Voltaire, such as the delicate lithograph *Pont Neuf* (1921; fig.23). The Tate catalogue describes how its 'linear rhythms of railings, steps, tree branches and the arches of the Pont Neuf, foreshadows the artist's later preoccupation with straight and curved lines'.[10] In another version of this work, a scallop-edged curtain drifts inwards with the breeze, revealing the river and bridge below. It is reminiscent of her frequent images of theatre boxes – such as *Bristol Hippodrome* (1918–19; fig.6) or *At the Globe Theatre, London* (1919) – in which patrons peer out from behind heavily brocaded drapes, eliciting the same tangible sense of excitement at a life beyond.

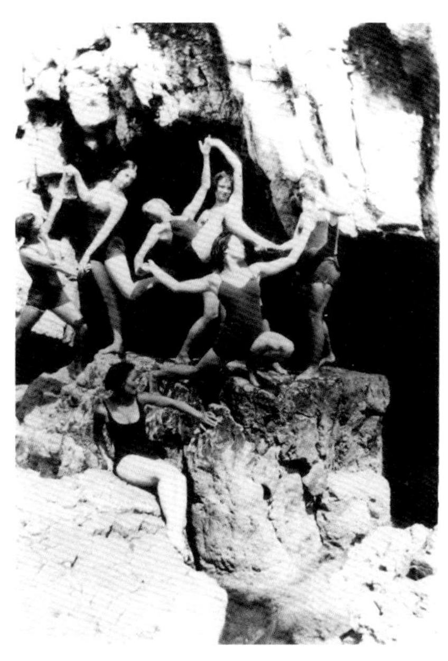

24
Dancers from Margaret Morris's summer dance school, Cap d'Antibes, c.1923–5, photograph by Paule Vézelay, 13.9 × 19.7 cm, Tate Archive

As Vézelay's black and white lines tentatively began to form new 'lives' in Paris, a trip in the summer of 1923 to Cap d'Antibes in the south of France (to which she returned in 1925) and an encounter with Margaret Morris's dance school set them firmly on their way. Among the decadent parties and masque balls, Vézelay's imagination was captured by Morris's modern dancers. Photographed gracefully bathing from the rocks and barefoot against a backdrop of heavily scented cypresses and pines, hands held high like church steeples, the expressive curves of their bodies breathed life into Vézelay's work. This can be seen in the rhythmic simplicity of *The Bathers* (1923; fig.25), a linocut featuring three groups of women with arms gently curved aloft, accentuating their sloping waistlines and rounded bellies against the undulating outline of the hills beyond. These overlapping lines reappear in the drypoint *Two Women* (1927; fig.27) and in numerous delicate pencil drawings of the time, reminiscent of Matisse's sylph-like women. With their carefully cut, curvilinear shapes, they precede the biomorphic forms that later float through charcoal skies; and her dancing figures provide choreography for her first defiant steps towards abstraction in works such as *White Shapes in Movement* (1930), *Personnage Tenant une Fleur* (1933) and *Dancing Forms* (1933; fig.28).

But before these lines could come to life, they first had to seek out a more vital component. In her early years in Paris Vézelay befriended a cast of performers from the fabled Cirque Medrano, providing the inspiration for a book of drawings and rhymes featuring Wallser the dancing horse, Madam Bella Blonda, White Wonder and the Acrogen Acrobats and Troop. Its opening verse declares: 'I give you a circus a ring a circle not a sphere.'[11] Despite the book's whimsy, these surprisingly revealing words introduce a missing facet later to prove of great importance to her work: that of three-dimensional space.

It is with this realisation that Vézelay begins to consider how she might join her lines in space – so that a circle can become a sphere. A work often cited as anticipating the series *Lines in Space* is the linocut *La Danseuse à la Corde* (1921; fig.29).[12] Sarah Wilson, an early champion, paints a vivid picture of the artist transfixed by the Medrano's tightrope walkers, as they teeter high above the audience below: 'One imagines her watching them dancing on those lines in space, pondering the precariousness of life and her future career.'[13] Just as Alexander Calder discovered 'drawing in space' with his miniature Cirque Calder, Vézelay also began to think of her lines inhabiting a third dimension. However, it was some time before her lines would leave the two-dimensional world, instead envisioning an 'impression of space' which 'although completely

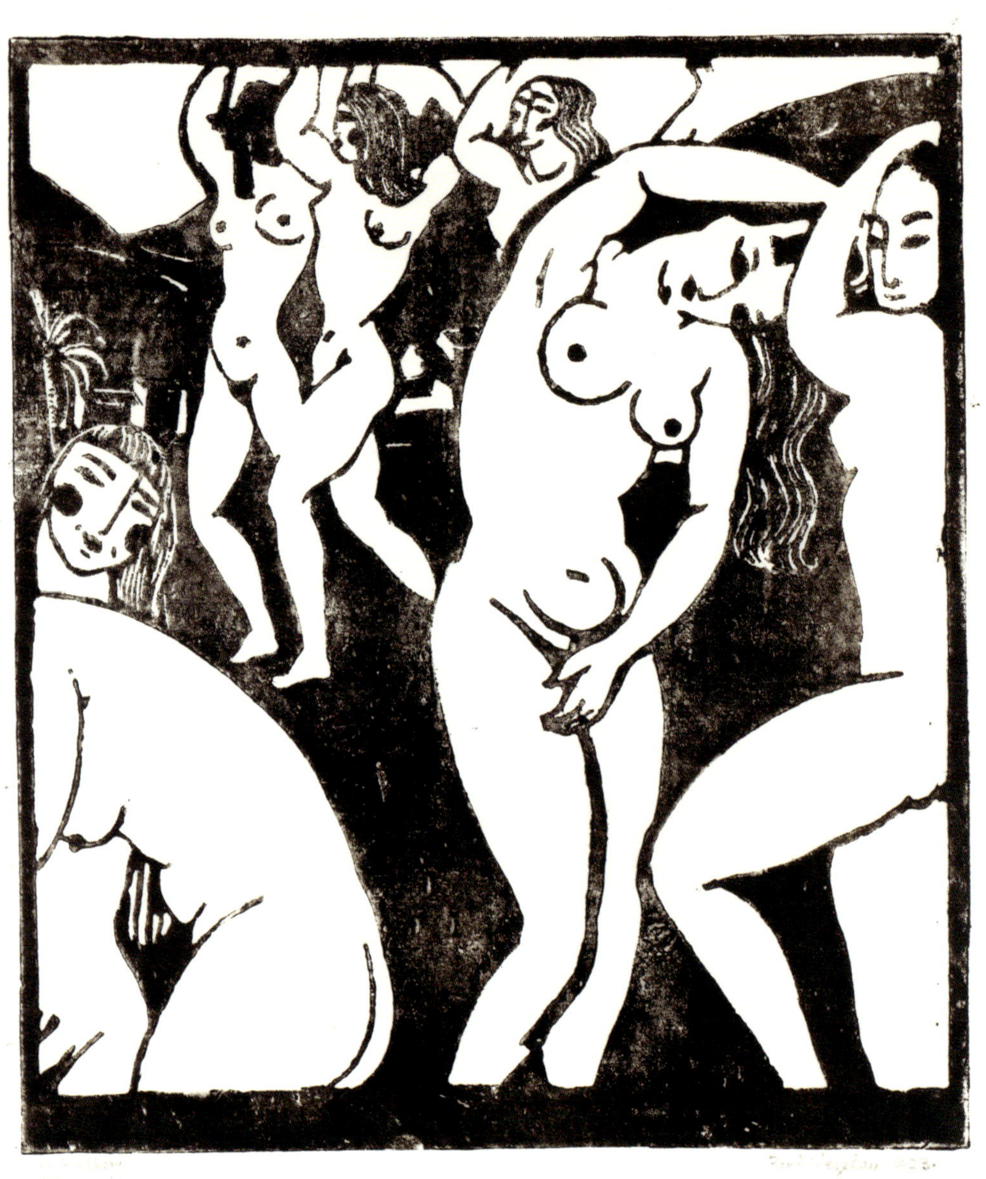

25
Marjorie Watson-Williams / Paule Vézelay,
The Bathers, 1923, linocut, 26.7 × 23.5 cm, Tate

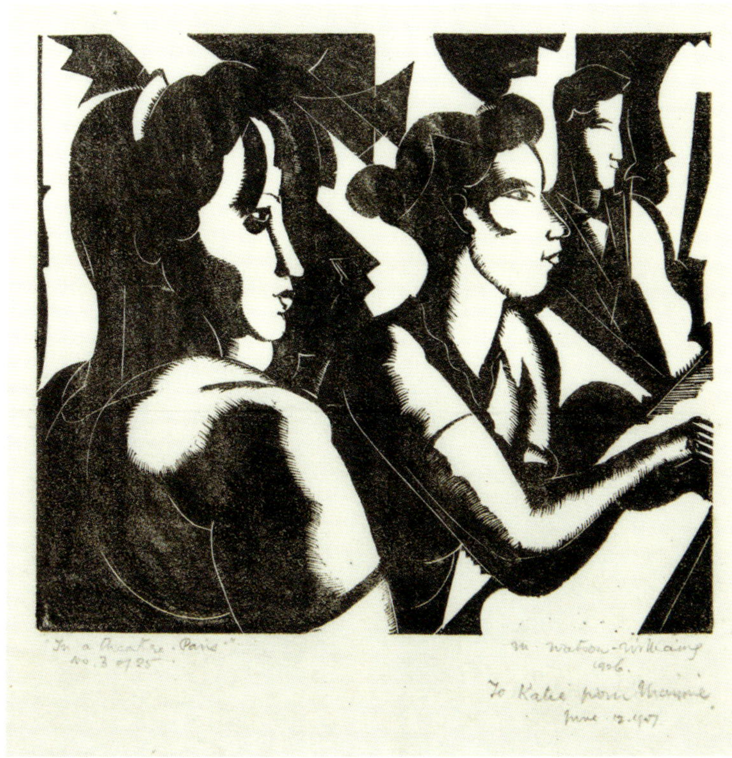

26
Marjorie Watson-Williams / Paule Vézelay,
In a Theatre, Paris, 1921, linocut, 12 × 14 cm,
Royal West of England Academy, Bristol

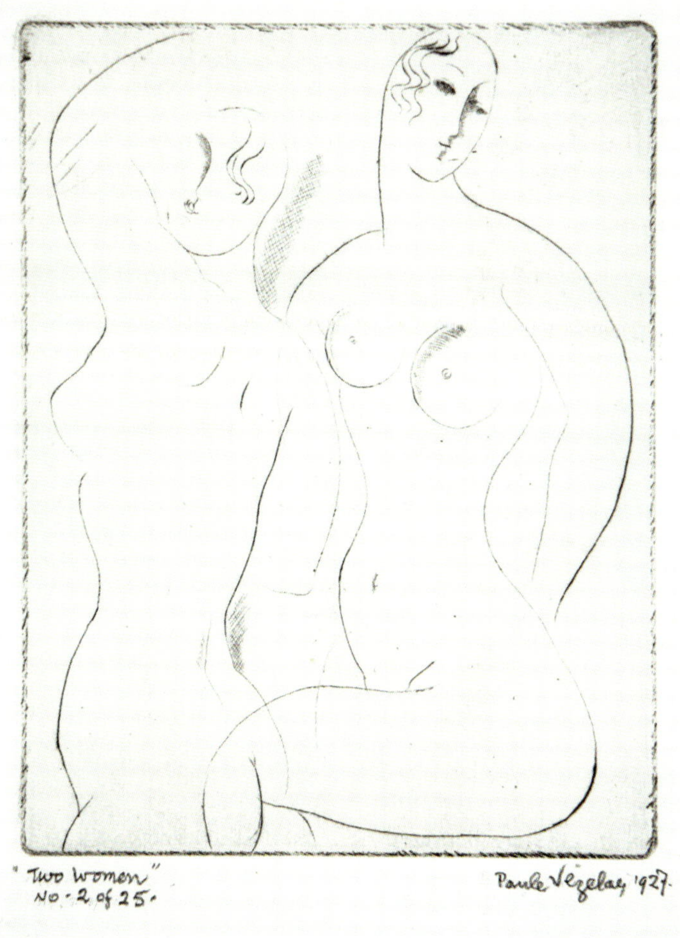

27
Paule Vézelay, *Two Women*, 1927, drypoint on
paper, 14.8 × 11.5 cm, England & Co.

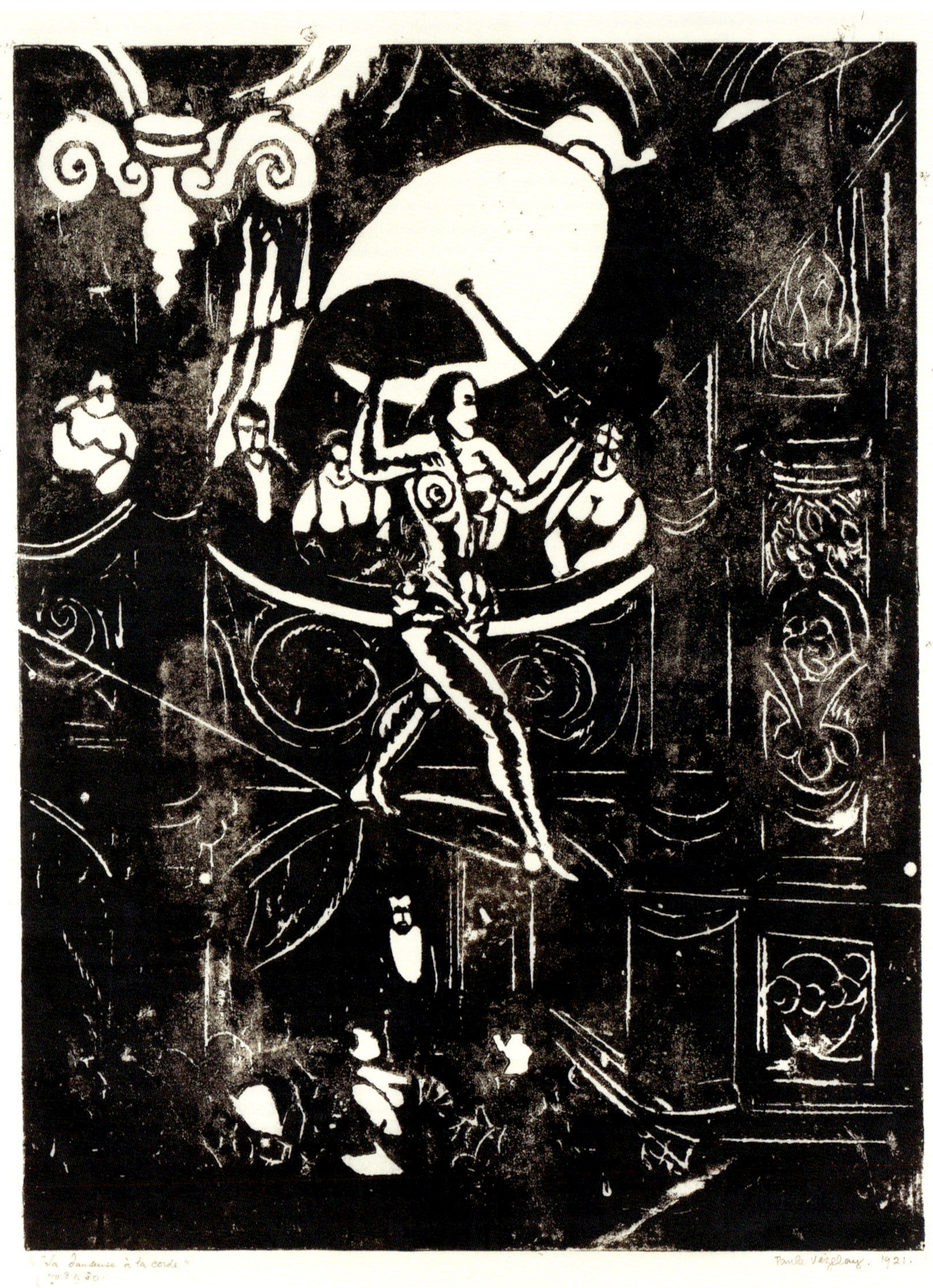

29
Marjorie Watson-Williams / Paule Vézelay, *La Danseuse à la Corde*, 1921, linocut, 39.1 × 30.5 cm, Tate

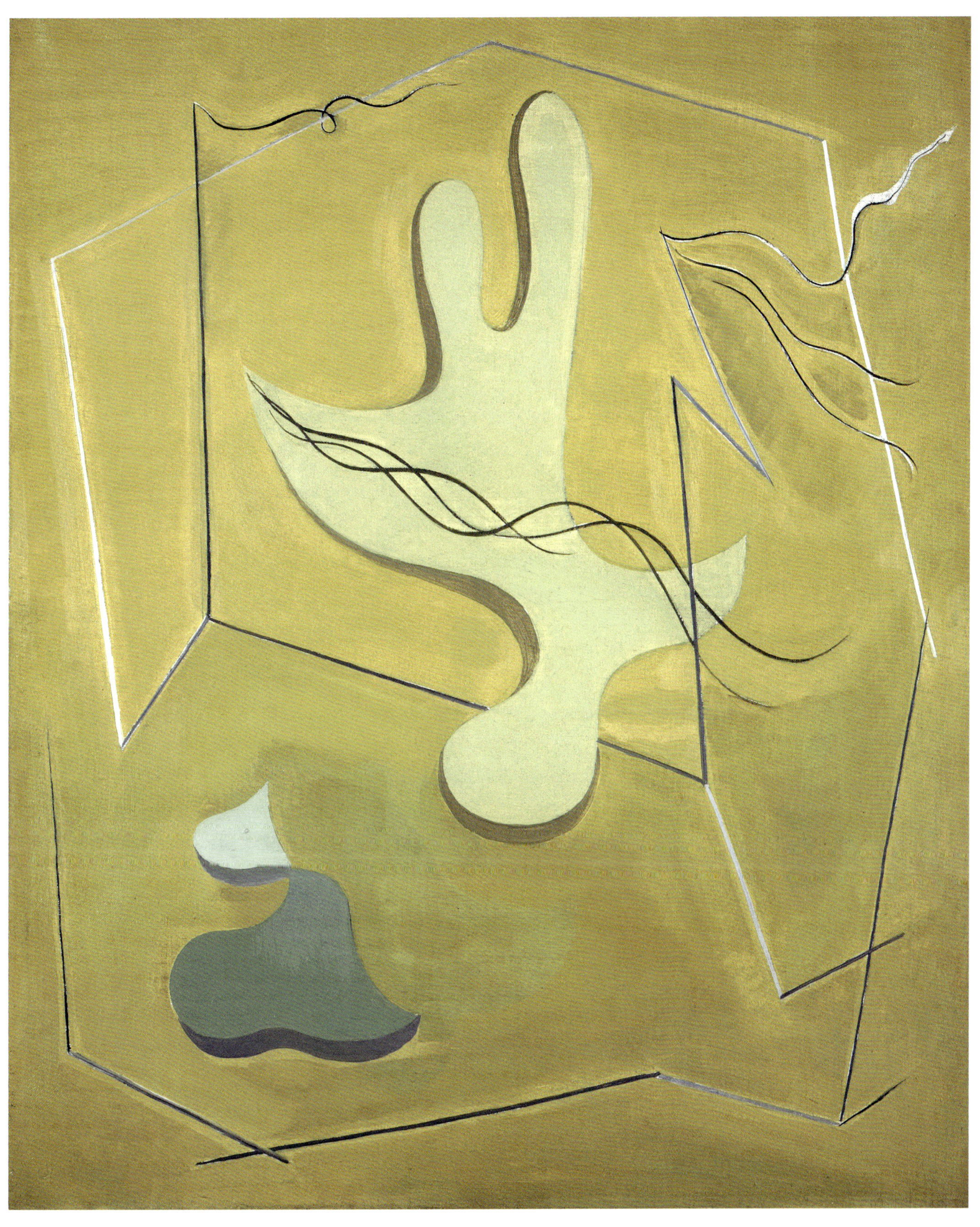

28
Paule Vézelay, *Dancing Forms*, 1933, oil on canvas, 55 × 46 cm, private collection

imaginary, can transform the flat surface into a space filled with light and air'.[14]

Excited by this new direction, in 1926 Vézelay settled in Paris, making the city at last her home. During this period she still remained concerned with her search for equilibrium, seeking an answer as to how an artist might solve 'the mathematical problem of balance and harmony while keeping his desires and his vision bright'.[15] Inspired by the performers with whom she had become familiar, Vézelay looked to the melodies with which Morris's dancers moved and the rhythm of Rimbaud's verse, finding their equivalent within the work of the painter Juan Gris. Writing about his valiant attempts to 'humanise painting', Vézelay found solace in another artist looking beyond harmonies in line and colour for an art less 'mental and geometrical' and more 'emotional and introspective' – searching for a 'beautiful song'.[16] Seeking this lyricism, the first tentative notes of a chord or steps of a dance can be seen seeping into Vézelay's work, as she hungrily drew upon influences from within the myriad of growing artistic movements flourishing among her contemporaries at the time.

Her first foray was a relatively brief flirtation with Surrealism, a period in which her lines began to embrace animation, encompassing both physical activation (through dance and music) and metaphorical movement. Vézelay was able to liberate her figurative lines so that they interacted, rather than simply overlapped, with one another. Released from their static positions, her lines began to jostle and hum in works such as *Walking in the Wind* (1930; fig.30), *The Bathers* (1930) and the aptly named *La Danse* (1931). She also adopted elements from André Masson's work, employing his 'characteristic zig-zag line' for her own effect.[17] This 'calligraphic' line has been described as a form of 'écriture', a French term that refers not only to the act of writing but to a stylistic impulse.[18] This urge is reminiscent of the 'inevitability' and wilful 'desire' with which Vézelay associates her lines. It also suggests a certain dynamism, an active exploration of movement inspired by the fluidity with which the Surrealists moved between the conscious and unconscious worlds.

After her separation from Masson in 1932, Vézelay's work once again changes shape. Wilson points to abstract works such as *Triangles and Tubes* (1932) as evidence of a new direction.[19] Abstraction had already begun to appear in works such as *Composition with Blue Vase and Table* (1928), yet it was not until 1934 that she joined the group Abstraction-Création, truly cementing her allegiances. However, despite an emphasis among some members on Constructivism, Concrete Art and Neoplasticism, Vézelay continued to take a more lyrical, organic approach, as seen in *Curves and Circles* (1930; fig.31), *White Shapes in Movement* (1930) and *Formes en Movement* (1933). Utilising her straight and curved lines and the dreamlike spaces of the Surrealists, she created her own form of abstraction, in which the curving lines of rivers, leaves and landscapes are given equal precedence as the taut edge of a tightrope.

Although still bound to the two-dimensional world, Vézelay's lines can now be felt starting to shift and lift with works such as *Triangle Holding a Sphere* (1933), in which shapes are no longer 'tied to "earth"', appearing instead 'to float in "natural space"'.[20] Both geometric and organic forms began to harmonise and exist together with a new-found ease, often credited to her growing and mutually inspirational friendship with the artists Jean Arp and Sophie Taeuber-Arp. In the catalogue for *Imagination, Mathematics and Balance* at the Zabriskie Gallery, New York, in 1988, Wilson describes a new-found sense of equilibrium in Vézelay's work: 'Rarely are her geometrical

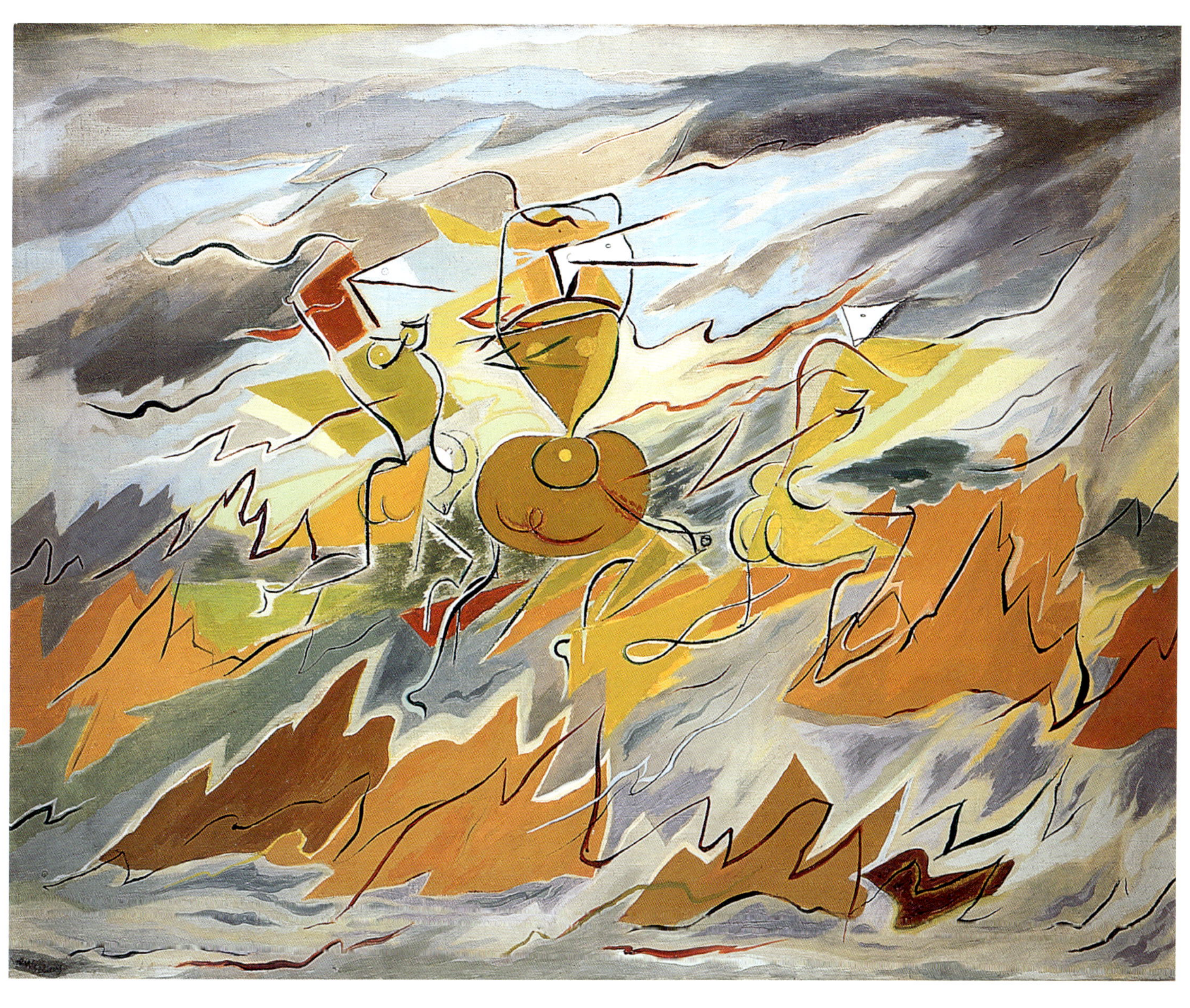

30
Paule Vézelay, *Walking in the Wind*, 1930, oil on canvas, 73 × 91.5 cm, England & Co.

forms so pure, her backgrounds so blank that they belong to the realm of mathematical reason alone. Inevitably, one reads life forms into her shapes, flatly arranged or mysteriously floating. Yet the hints of tenderness, of playfulness, in her biomorphic lines and forms, can be instantly tautened into non-emotive geometries. Pure reason and will thus balance desire.'[21] Wilson attributes this to Arp's influence, while elsewhere she identifies Taeuber-Arp's 'lightness and dancing quality' as another key influence on Vézelay's work.

Vézelay absorbed these new elements into her visual language alongside a growing interest in sculpture, which 'increased my knowledge of form and its relation to space'.[22] Balancing purity of form with a dance-like playfulness, she was now able to form her own response to Abstraction's call for the creation of a 'new universe, the universe of human imagination'.[23] Stepping inside this world, she would finally 'free her lines'. Much as she had embraced the make-believe world of theatre and suspended belief at acrobatic feats in the circus ring, she addressed her own self-imposed limitations to ask: why should lines in art be confined to two-dimensional space while 'ordinary lines outside the realm of art, enjoyed freedom in space'?[24]

It was in this spirit that, in 1935, Vézelay made her three-dimensional constructions, devising a wooden case and using stretched fishing wire, cotton threads or fine cord to create straight lines. These became known as her *Recherches en trois dimensions, tableaux de fils et ficelles tendus*,[25] the tentative beginnings of what she considered her most original artistic achievement. They were first shown at the Galerie Jeanne Bucher-Myrbor in 1937. The exhibition catalogue contains a drawing by Vézelay of ten different groups of lines, some intersecting, some running in parallel, an embodiment of her 'living lines'.

These imaginative works later became known as her *Lines in Space*, with new and frequent adaptations introduced throughout her lifetime. In the 1960s these included organic shapes cut out of wood, as in *Construction No.43: Four Silhouettes* (1964; fig.50) and *Lines in Space No.51* (1965), as well as the complete removal of outer boxes to create freestanding sculptures with looped wires, such as *Lines in Space No.53* (1965; fig.34), which could be seen as a three-dimensional version of the emblematic *Portrait of a Line* (1944). Also, not to be forgotten, are the plaster sculptures she developed alongside her early constructions, such as *Garden* (1935; fig.16), *Five Forms* (1935) and *Dish and Little Boat* (1935–6); each of these creations could be seen as its own microcosmic universe of 'human imagination'.

However, it was with the replacement early on of thread and string by wire (aiding the creation of both curved and straight lines) that she introduced a vital and final element to her work: 'So it was that with stretched threads and curved wires I had my two lines, the Straight line and the Curved line, composed in the element of Space. My "Lines in Space" created a third element by casting their shadows, and these changing delicate echoes seemed to add depth and light and beauty to the whole construction. They had, as all shadows have for me, a quality of magic.'[26]

An interest in lighting and shadows exists throughout Vézelay's work. She often suggested that the play between light and dark cast upon the seated audience was where her real interest in the theatre lay, even going as far as to make enquiries to study the craft of theatrical lighting. Likewise, her archive contains numerous black and white photographs of her three-dimensional work, often captured at different angles to see how the light would fall. These

31
Paule Vézelay, *Curves and Circles*, 1930, oil on canvas, 92 × 73 cm, Tate

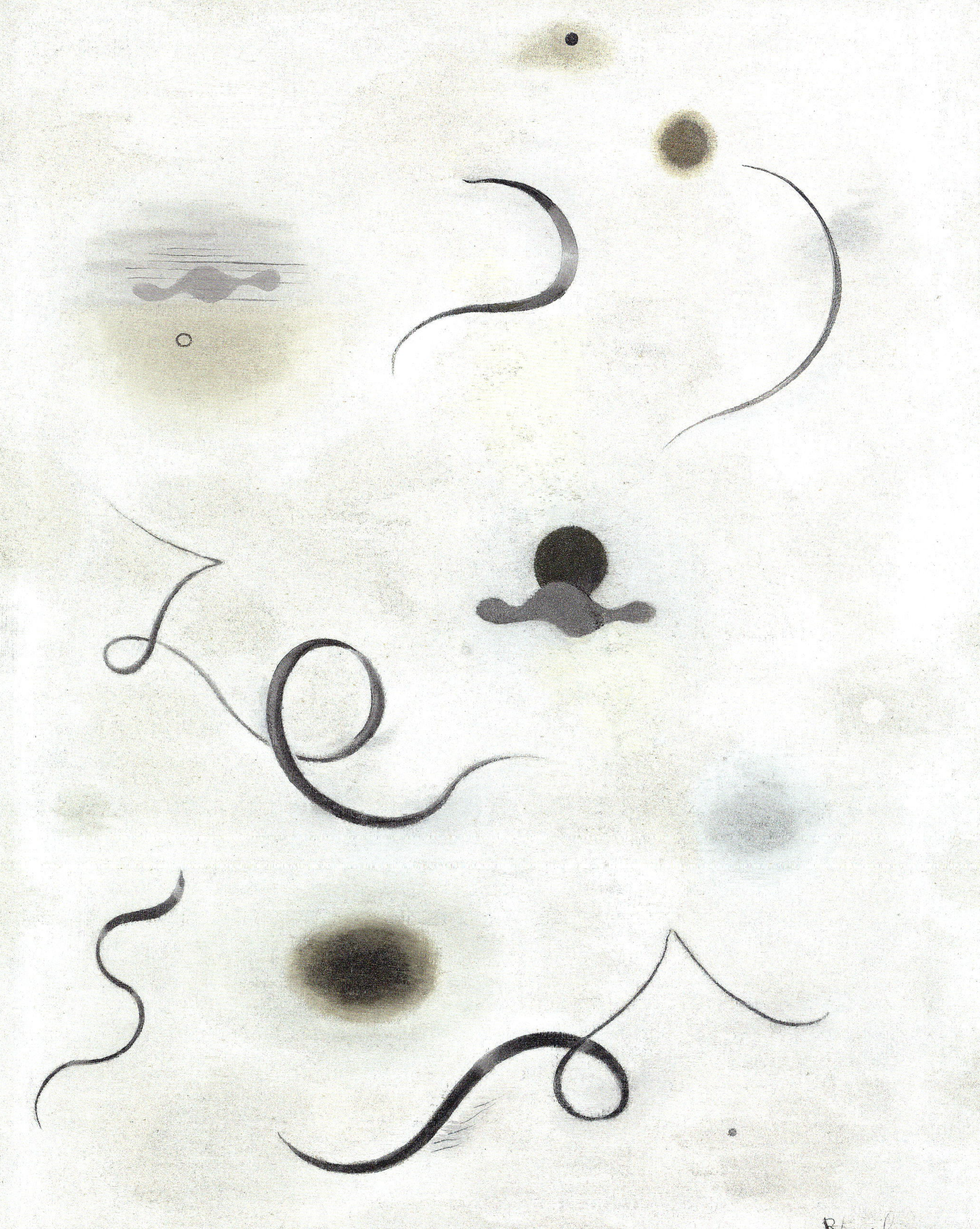

32
Paule Vézelay, *Lines in Space No.3*, 1936, cotton threads and canvas on board, 71 × 62 × 12 cm, Tate

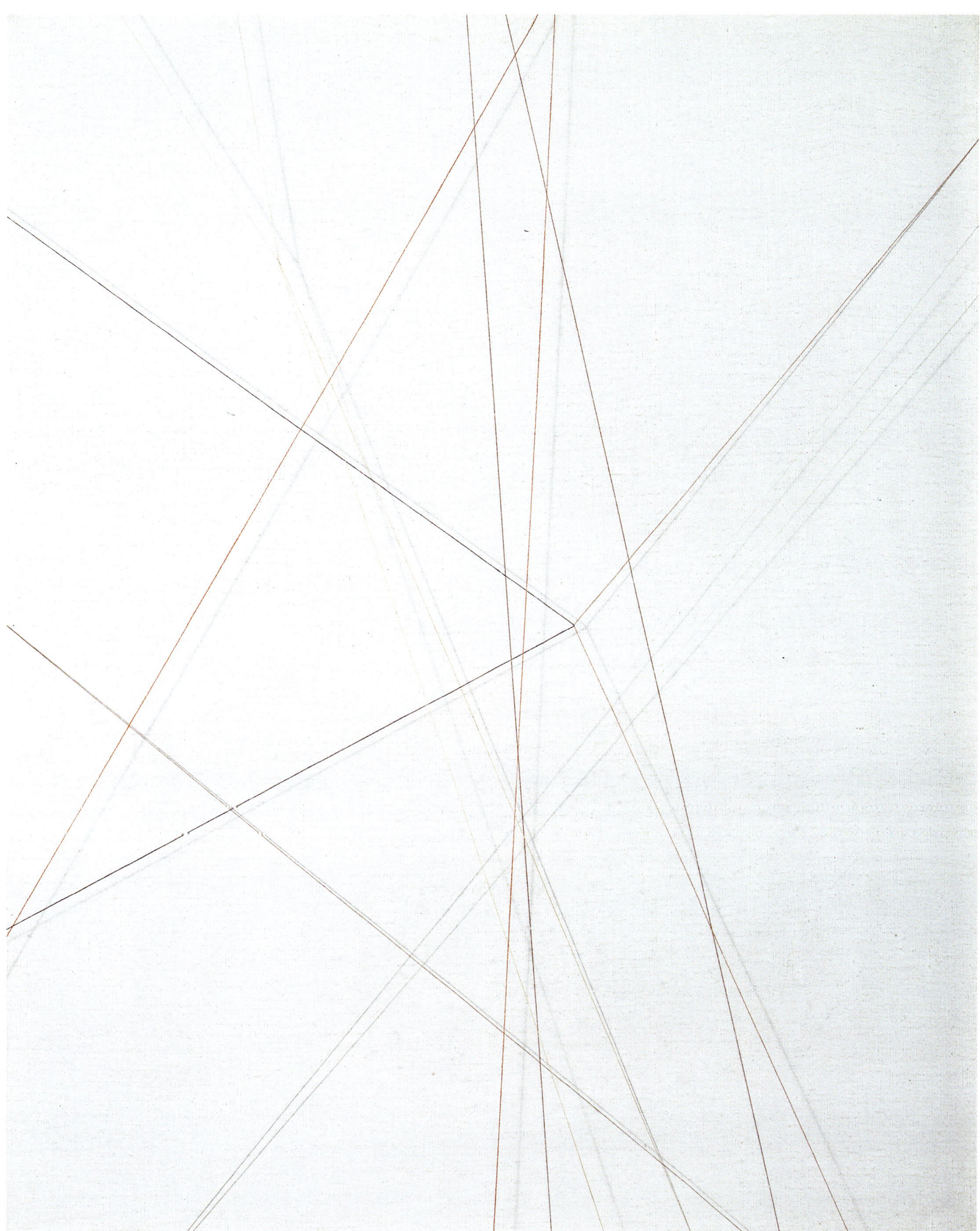

33
Paule Vézelay, *Construction with Nine Forms in Wood on White Ground*, 1964, wood construction, 47.5 × 45 cm, private collection

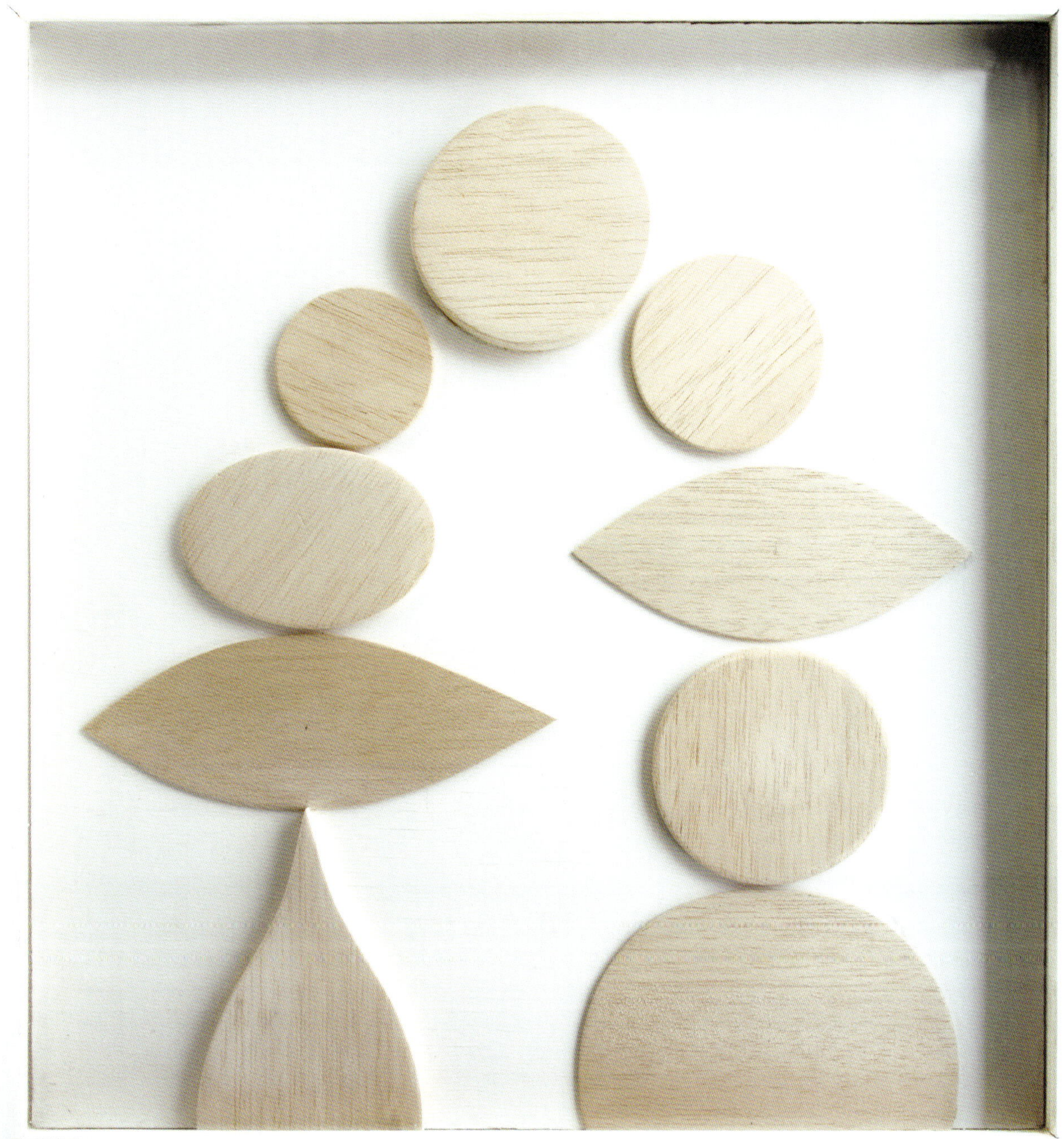

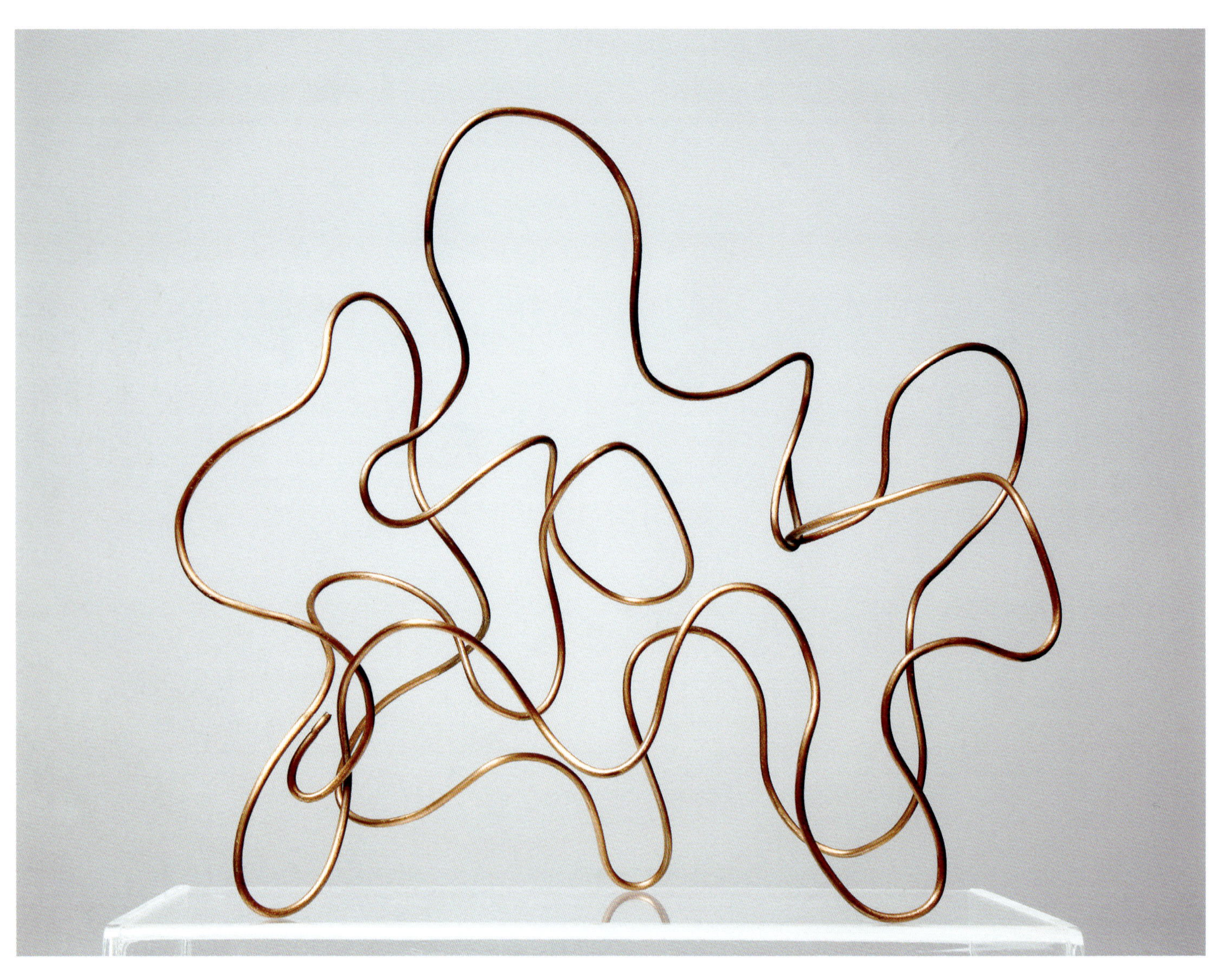

34
Paule Vézelay, *Lines in Space No.53*, 1965,
wire construction, 22 × 28 × 12 cm, private collection

are accompanied by exercise books filled with handwritten notes carefully recording the focal lengths and shutter speeds with which each image was captured. Among these notes are also, fascinatingly, ideas for experiments in photographing her plaster sculptures, using red and green lights, a mobile stand and a motor, to capture varying effects of colour, movement and shadow.

Vézelay's interest in shadows can be traced back to childhood and her mother's collection of silhouettes and painted profiles of ancestors, which held a great attraction for her. In an unpublished essay, 'Meandering with Two Mediums' (1970), she recalls using them as inspiration for a book of short stories; and although abandoned for a period, her interest was reignited in the 1930s, when she was asked to make hand-block-printed textile designs for a French company.[27] Using coloured paper, she replaced her pencil with scissors, bringing these cut lines to life. She used this technique for many years in her textile designs, accumulating box upon box filled with fragments of coloured paper, tracing paper, balsa wood and card – shapes and lines which she believed each had their own individual 'lives'.

Given her many triumphs across different mediums, encompassing drawing, printmaking, painting, sculpture and textiles, Vézelay's parting wish was to be known as the first British abstract artist and a true 'Master of Line'.[28] Yet this desire for precedence and mastery belies the magic with which she sought to imbue her work and her world. It has been suggested that Rimbaud's imagined scenes embodied a sense of freedom that spoke to Vézelay, fuelling her own attempt at liberating her treasured lines. Therefore, how better to remember her work, from the meandering rivers to lines in space, than through 'the harmony of music' and 'the rhythm of poetry'[29] in the realm of make-believe, in which reality is suspended and reason and imagination sit in perfect harmony, and where among the 'delicate echoes' of shadows Vézelay's lines are brought to life. And they dance.

35
Paule Vézelay, *Lines in Space, No. 11*, 1960,
cotton and nylon thread box construction,
24 × 35 cm, private collection

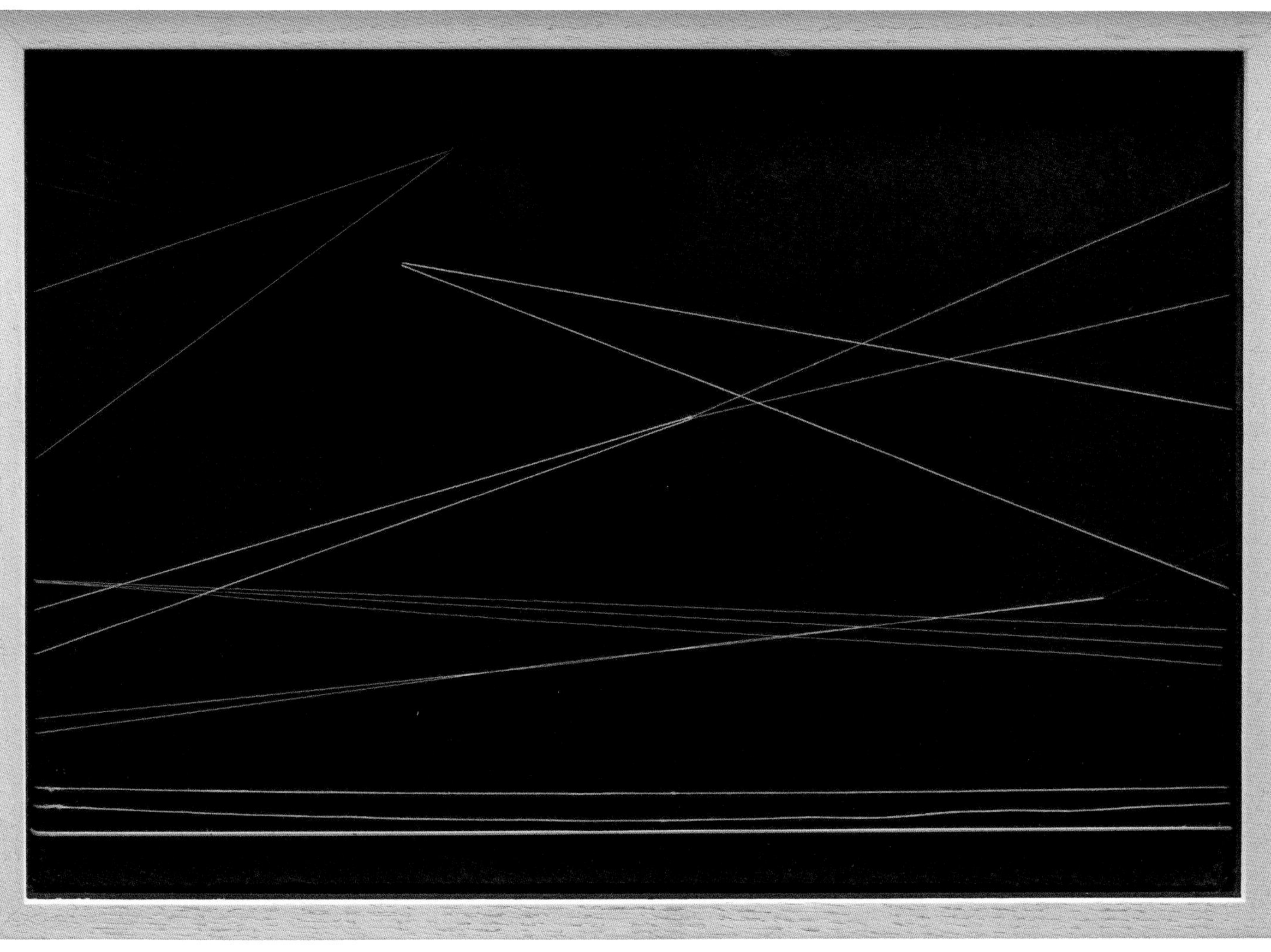

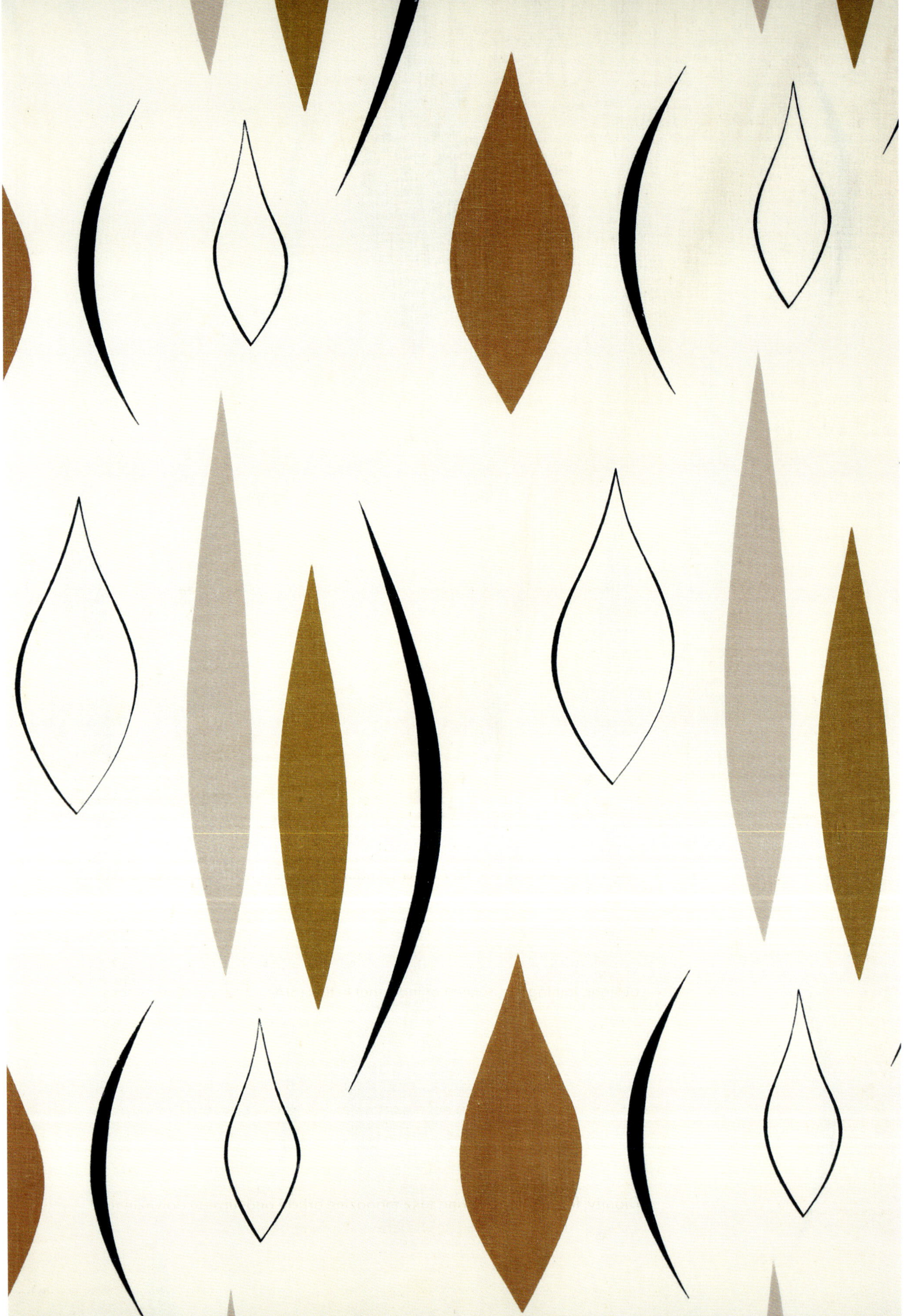

Textile Designs

> *Heal's asked me to design for them and I enjoyed it very much . . . if it's well done, when the curtains are drawn . . . it breaks up the design in a most interesting way.*[1]

Vézelay began designing printed textiles towards the end of the Second World War in order to supplement her modest private income, at a time when she was living between England and Paris. In 1945 gallerist Jeanne Bucher introduced her to Jean Bauret, whose firm, La Société Industrielle de la Lys, had commissioned a textile design from Kandinsky. Responding to her letter enclosing a drawing, he wrote, 'And the architectural point of view governs all, your project moreover isn't architectural enough, like, by the way, Kandinsky's which Madame Bucher showed you realised in fabric.'[2] Heeding this advice, Vézelay sold Bauret six designs in 1946 – three variations on a ribbon-like snake, similar to her 1944 drawing *Portrait of a Line*; some curved, crossing, seaweed-like forms, echoing her drawings of Second World War bomb damage in Bristol; and a geometric, shuttle-like motif – and in 1947 the geometric *Lettres Imaginaires*.[3] This constituted Vézelay's apprenticeship in textile design. Extant samples suggest that all six designs were produced, and the shuttle-motif fabric was illustrated in the May 1950 edition of *The Ambassador*, a British export trade magazine founded by the well-connected Hans and Elsbeth Juda.

Between 1945 and 1947 Vézelay designed a screen-printed silk headsquare and rayon dress fabric for Ascher (London) Ltd, again having been introduced by Bucher.[4] Both prints are delicate and feminine without being overly pretty, owing to the assortment of intriguing Surrealist motifs. Considerable interest was shown in the many prints commissioned by Ascher from modern artists.[5]

Vézelay made a concerted effort to find London buyers for furnishing fabric designs, joining the Society of Industrial Artists (SIA) in 1949. In summer 1953 David Whitehead Ltd, the leading manufacturer of affordable contemporary printed furnishing fabrics, commissioned two designs, one of which was produced and appeared in a feature on the manufacturer in the April 1954 issue of *The Ambassador*. The article celebrated the exhibition *The Ambassador* had sponsored in the autumn of 1953 at the Institute of Contemporary Art, *Painting into Textiles*, which increased British artists' subsequent involvement in textile design and was 'of seminal importance in this development, of what was essentially a new aesthetic'.[6] Vézelay's elegant, softly curving linear design, *Dignity*, featured in a spring 1954 magazine article and (upside down) in the windows of a house in the 1956 *Ideal Home Exhibition*.[7]

36
Paule Vézelay, *Crescents*, 1954, roller-printed cotton, Estate of Paule Vézelay

In 1954 Vézelay sold two designs to Metz & Co, the leading Dutch textile manufacturer, which had commissioned designs from Delaunay.[8] These comprised a geometric pattern of columns of crossing lines, reminiscent of her linear designs for Bauret and the *vernissage* invitation she designed for her 1937 exhibition at the Galerie Jeanne Bucher-Myrbor; and a pattern combining biomorphic shapes and curved lines, resembling her earlier *Lines in Space* constructions.

In 1950 Lucienne Day, in her capacity as SIA Honorary Secretary, had invited Vézelay to submit designs for Heal's and Hambro's, New York. Hambro's selected two designs, but Vézelay demurred. She explained in a 1953 letter seeking commissions from Tom Worthington, a design consultant at Heal's, which had started manufacturing its own fabrics in 1946: 'I did not care to let them go out to the USA unless sold. I work almost entirely to commission and for that reason I am not able to leave my designs with producers.'[9] Following Worthington's eventual visit to her studio in May 1954, she confirmed his requirements. 'I understand you want a free and "flowing" design rather than a geometrical one.'[10] *Crescents* is a fresh, crisp combination of solid and linear curved geometric forms in clear but not over-bright colours, which appear to move upwards. Thus commenced Vézelay's most significant design partnership, building on her initial successes.

The Heal's annual review of sales led to unsuccessful designs and colourways (i.e. the combination of colours in which fabric is printed) being discontinued. Analysis of the annual wholesale price lists for roller-printed cottons enables assessment of the longevity and relative success of Vézelay's fabrics compared with those of other Heal's designers during the period. At the time of Vézelay's first Heal's commission, Day was their leading printed textile designer, working with them until 1970. In 1956 and 1959 Day had 18 designs in production, the highest number of any designer for the period of 1956 to 1970. Day had specialised in textile design at the Royal College of Art. Like Vézelay, she complained about her early experience of designing for Manchester manufacturers, saying that if she did sell a design, she lost control over the repeat and colourways, or it was not produced. This led her to sell designs only on commission. Day's well-known 1951 *Calyx* design helped revolutionise British printed furnishing fabric in the shift from utility designs to what became the British Contemporary style, remaining in production until 1955.[11]

Although tremendously prolific, also designing textiles and related products for other companies, Day said, 'It isn't an easy process . . . It doesn't roll out like it does with some designers – I have to work at it.'[12] Similarly, according to Vézelay, 'to draw a line is very difficult. It takes years before you can draw the exact line you want in the exact way in the exact place that you want it to be, with its modulations of tone, curves and so on. It's not all that easy.'[13] Unlike Day, Vézelay had no assistant and sometimes bemoaned the time involved in preparing colourways and large repeats.[14] Worthington responded: 'few firms would take so much trouble about the colourways and take time to check over each colourway, but I can assure you that the bigger percentage of our designers and artists do no less in this direction than you do.'[15] Vézelay approached her textile designs as seriously as her fine art and felt she deserved to be remunerated accordingly, despite the low status of textile designers.[16] In 1955 she raised her fee for Heal's in accordance with the SIA scale, charging an additional percentage for each colourway, and in 1956 she did so without

37
Paule Vézelay, *Elegance*, 1955, roller-printed cotton, Estate of Paule Vézelay

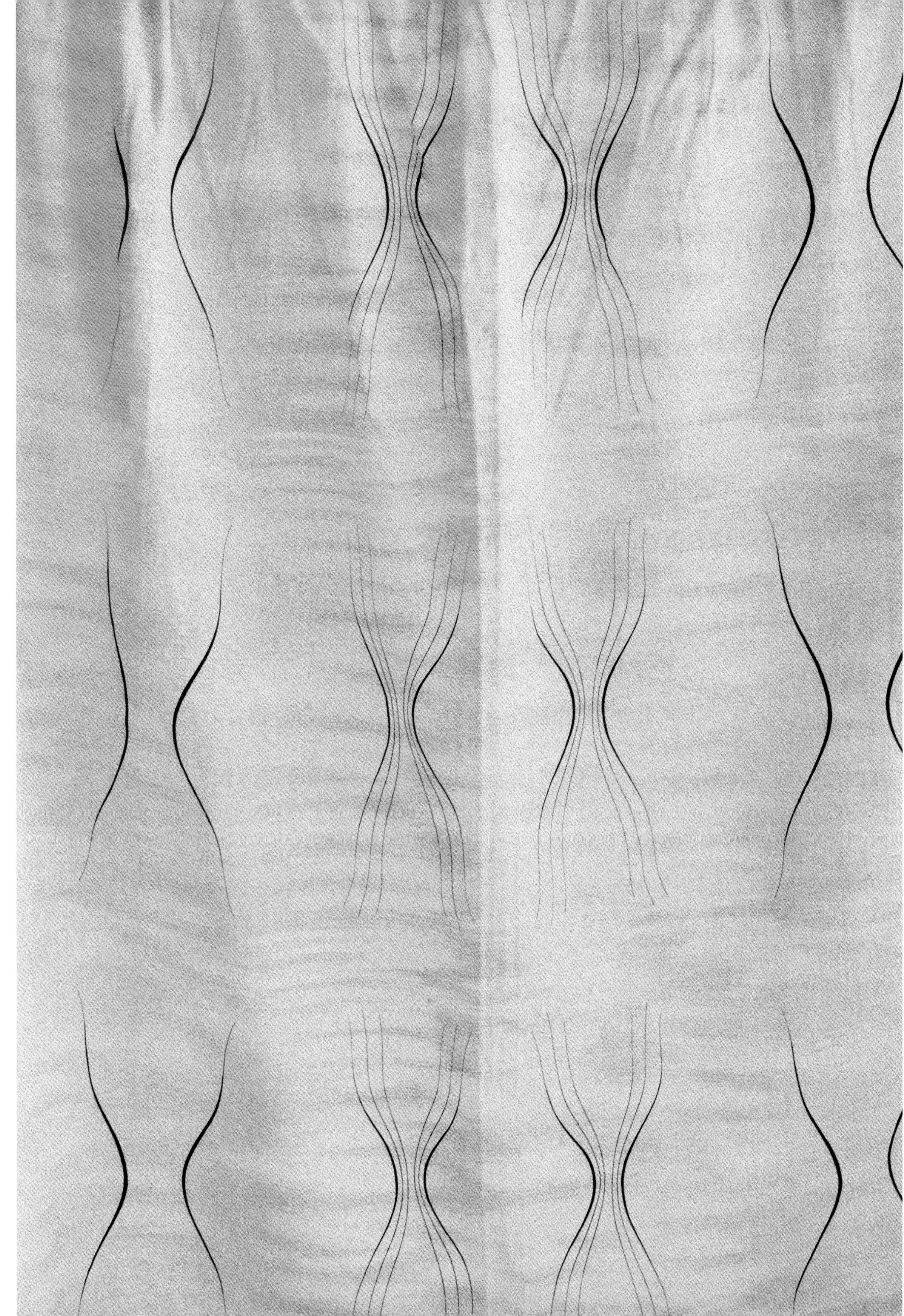

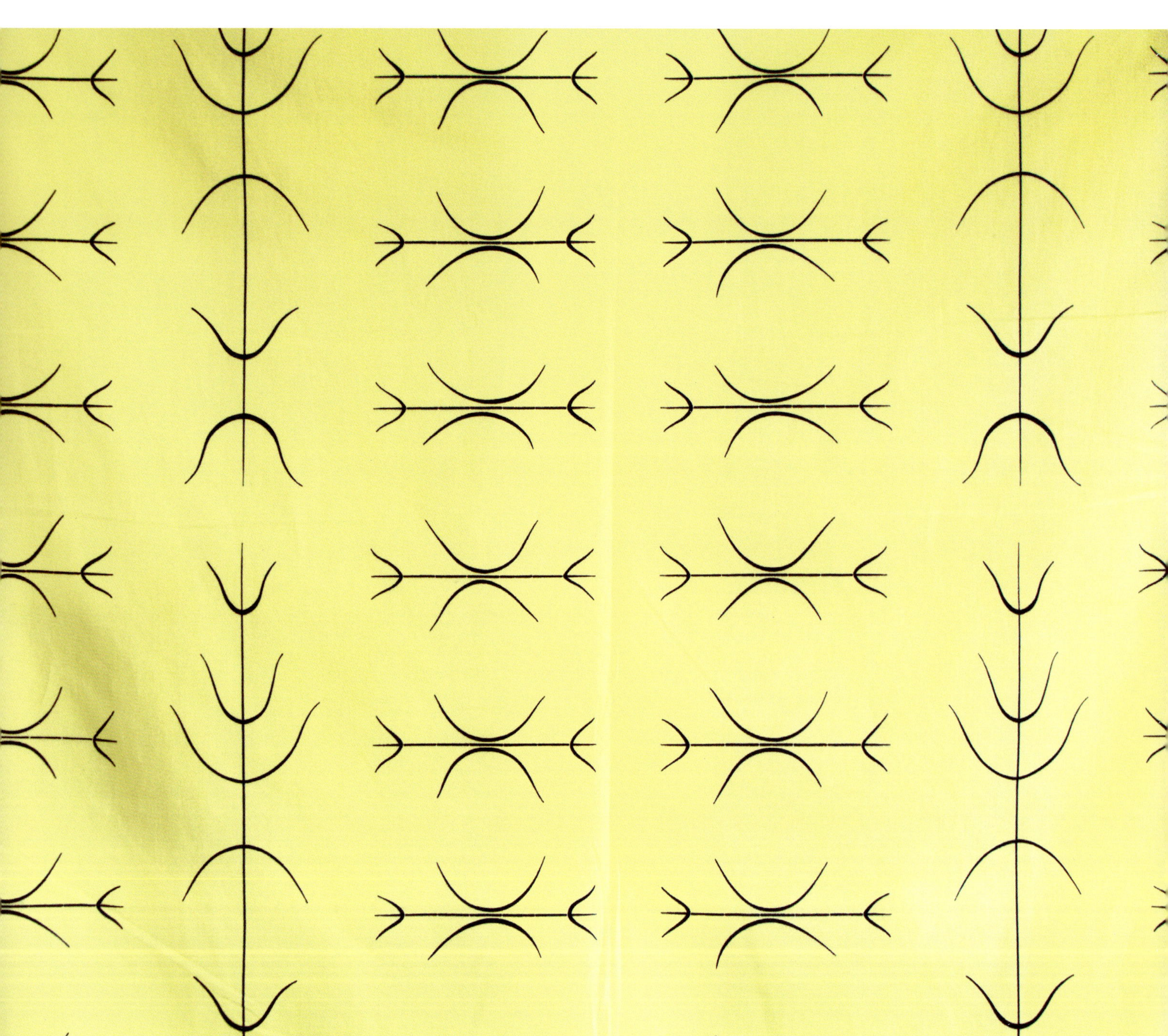

38
Paule Vézelay, *Perception*, 1961, roller-printed cotton, Estate of Paule Vézelay

prior agreement.[17] Worthington reluctantly agreed to pay the sums requested, on the second occasion saying, 'this is much more than we pay any other designer, including Lucienne Day, and at least four times the average fee'.[18] Unlike Whitehead, Heal's had no internal design studio, giving Vézelay more control over the design process but exacerbating her disappointment when designs she sold were not produced.

Of the 27 designs Vézelay sold to Heal's from 1954 to 1967, 15 went into production. Her most successful years were 1959 and 1962, when she had seven designs in production, placing her among their top five designers during the period, the others being Day, Barbara Brown, Doreen Dyall and Peter Hall, all vocational designers. Nearly half the designers commissioned by Heal's had only one design produced. In 1969, Vézelay sought to increase her fees further, to reflect the size and complexity of the designs now required, and to impose a time limit on Heal's copyright.[19] This caused Worthington to end the relationship, probably because he now had his pick of vocational designers producing a wide variety of modern patterns, at a point when 'artists had largely disengaged with textile design'.[20]

Elegance, Vézelay's second Heal's design, was her most successful, remaining in production for seven years, and in 1956 it was exhibited both in Oslo and at *Designers in Britain*.[21] The pattern comprises two alternating motifs of black curving lines, resembling female torsos or vases against a mottled backdrop, giving the impression of forms floating in a landscape. The varying width of the tapering lines and the striated background convey shimmering movement, the muted colourways enhancing the subtle effect. The quality of the roller printing is as refined as screen printing. Vézelay's other linear design for Heal's was the 1961 *Perception*, in which larger and smaller abstract motifs are arranged at right angles to each other in columns on a solid-coloured background, recalling Vézelay's 1941 charcoal drawing *Winter*. On more than one occasion Vézelay expressed the wish to change from cut-outs to more linear designs, apparently to generate fresh ideas, but *Perception* was in production for only one year.

Vézelay's other Heal's designs may be divided into four groups: curved cut-outs; organic cut-outs; straight-sided cut-outs; and one-off designs inspired by nature.

Curved Cut-Outs

Contrasts and *Variations* were designed in 1956; *Composure* was designed in 1967. *Contrasts* is an all-over pattern comprising a dumbbell and circle motif in two sizes. *Composure* uses similar dumb-bell and circle motifs on a larger scale in a horizontal arrangement divided by a wide, wavy line, a design which repeats well across a draped curtain. The pattern echoes motifs in Vézelay's 1936 painting *Forms*. *Variations* uses two abstracted candlestick motifs arranged in an undulating line across the fabric width, the wave pattern highlighted by a circle under one of the motifs and an up-curving crescent under the other. Vézelay viewed the circle as stabilising a painting's composition.

Organic Cut-Outs

Harmony was designed in 1955; *Duet* and *Modulation* were designed in 1963. *Harmony*, a new departure for both Vézelay and Heal's, has a large form composed of two crossing leafy curves above a single, shallower leafy curve.

The upper form of the abstract motif resembles a cup and saucer and floats above another inverted saucer, but it is rescued from domesticity by sharing the silhouette of a skull and crossbones. *Duet*'s spiky, double-pineapple-crown motif is arranged in four columns across the width, separated by compound vertical stripes. When two or more lengths are joined together, there is a double stripe of each colour, preventing it from becoming strident. *Modulation* has a continuous vertical motif resembling a climbing plant, repeating four times across the fabric width, alternately reversed and separated by two thin vertical stripes, which disappear when the curtain is opened.

Straight-Sided Cut-Out Forms

There are four straight-sided cut-out patterns: *Elation*, *Parade* and *Pennons*, designed in 1957; and *Stanza*, designed in 1958. *Elation* has striking fish-like motifs moving in formation, like boats or aircraft, and was produced only once. *Pennons*, a sparser design with small triangular motifs positioned apparently at random across the fabric, like determined bunting, fared better, with two colourways in production for three years. *Parade* was equally successful, having an all-over pattern of spindle-like abstract motifs in two colours, inspired by magnified atoms, arranged in differently-sized columns.[22] This group of designs pointed the way to the ubiquitous larger-scale designs in bolder colours of the 1960s.

A photograph published in *The Ambassador* featuring *Parade* and *Stanza* was reprinted in the Heal's 1959 'Report and Accounts', showing the growing importance for the firm of contract furnishing, for which striking, larger-scale architectural designs, such as Vézelay's, were better suited than Day's domestic-scale designs. *Stanza* has bold, interrupted stripes in a staggered arrangement, perfect for large windows, somewhat resembling Barbara Hepworth's 1937 *Pillar* design for Edinburgh Weavers. *Stanza* was in production for four years, to be succeeded by Day's similar 1967 *Causeway*, which also figured in Heal's promotional literature. Vézelay used *Stanza* fabric for her own sitting-room curtains.[23]

One-Off Designs Inspired by Nature

Froth and *Meander*, designed in 1960 and less abstract than Vézelay's other patterns, were both in production for two years. Her alternative names for *Froth* were 'Frivolity' and 'Sea Lace', the latter acknowledging the marine quality of the motifs, which also resemble her 1959 painting *Fragments and Circles*. *Meander*, originally commissioned by Metz & Co. but produced by Heal's, has a watery quality and depth.[24]

The period between the two world wars had seen the rise of elite artist-designed textiles. Vézelay was fortunate in entering the field at a time when good design was becoming democratised in the wake of the 1946 *Britain Can Make It* exhibition, which, despite its shortcomings, piqued public interest in 'design'.[25] Vézelay's textile designs demonstrate variety and owe their unique appeal to her artistic journey from representation through Surrealism to her own voice in non-figurative art. Coming to textile design late, without specific training or experience, gave rise to difficulties, but the support of Worthington and others enabled her to devise original patterns in accordance with her artistic principles.

39
Paule Vézelay, *Composure*, 1967, roller-printed cotton, Estate of Paule Vézelay

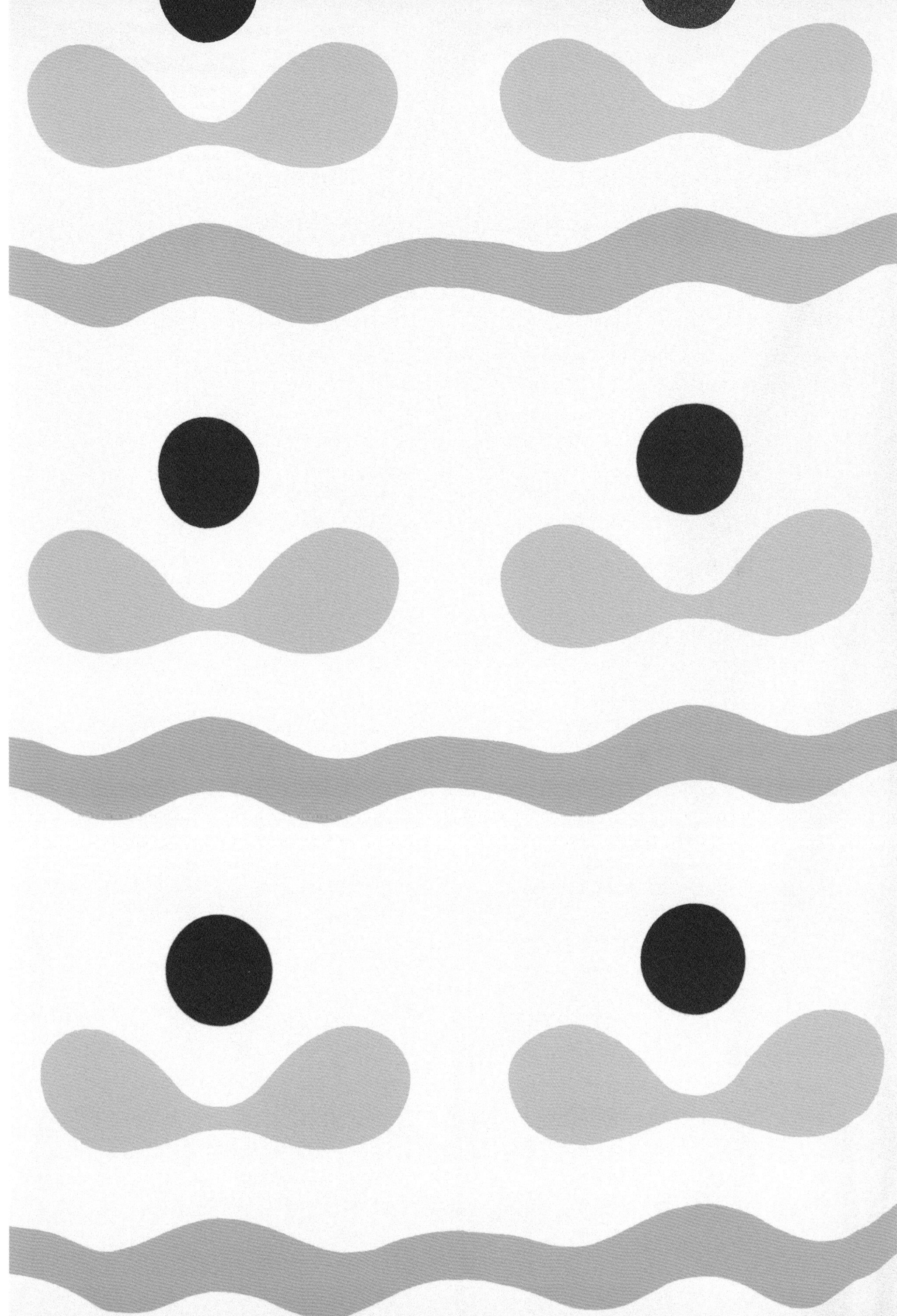

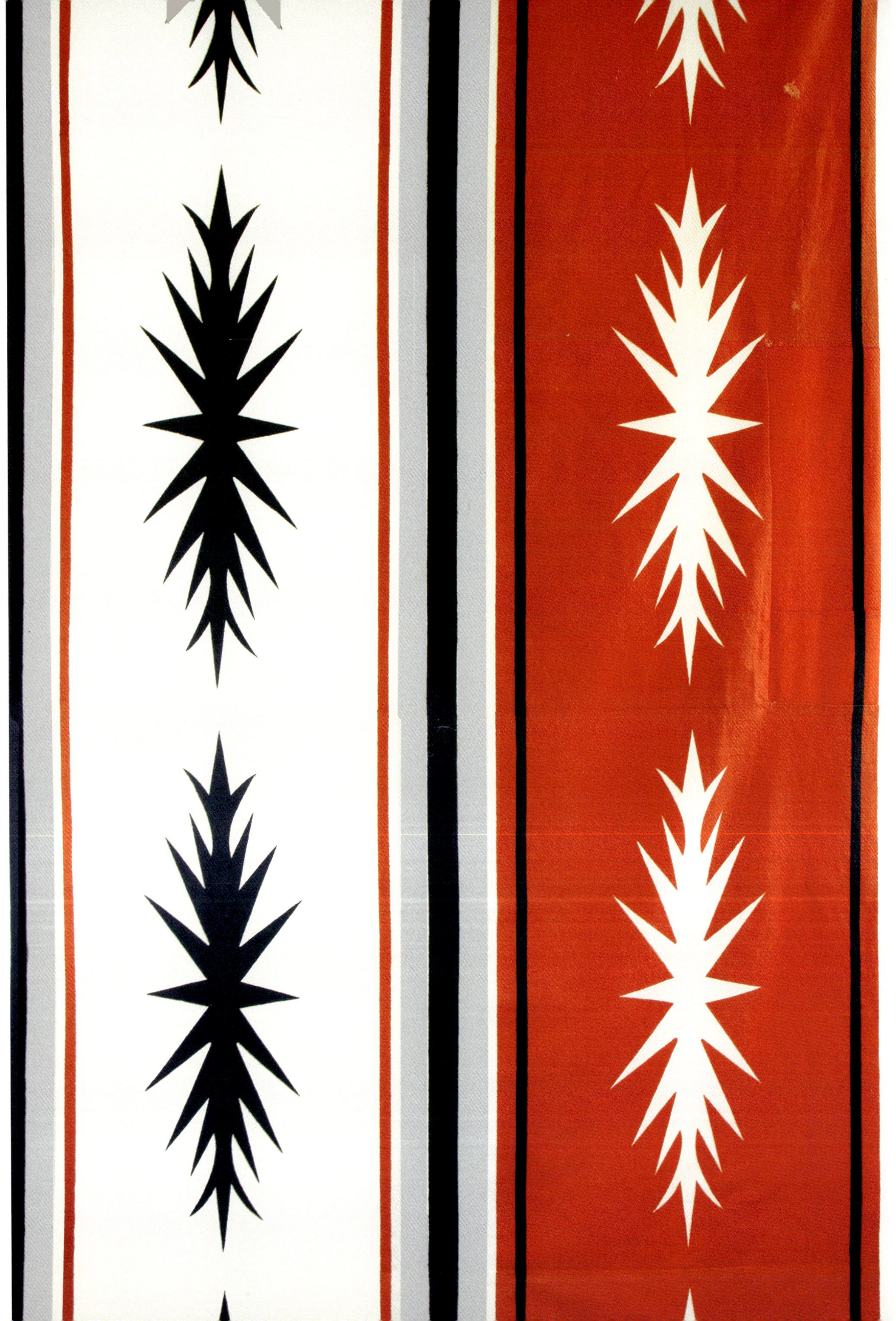

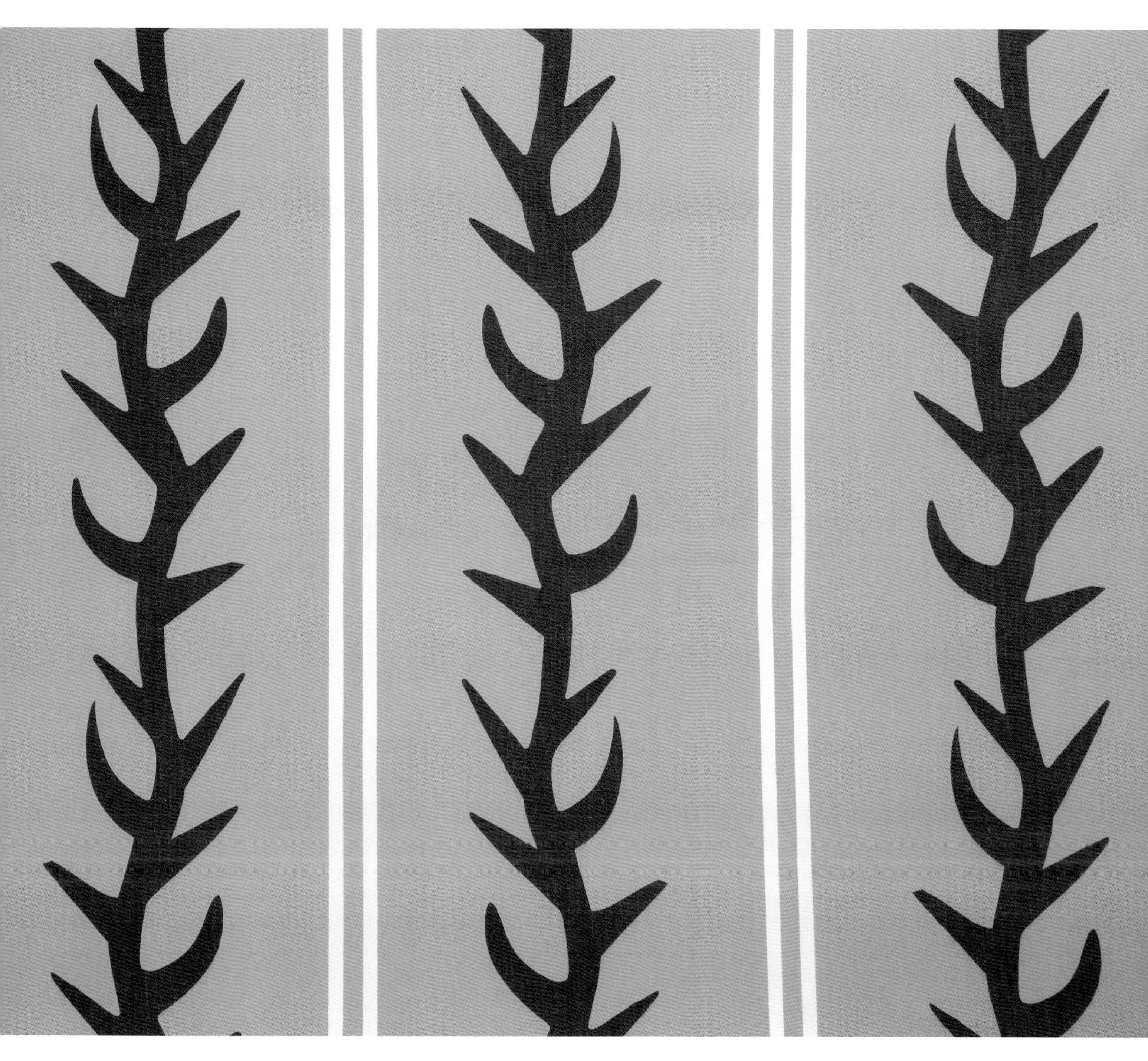

40
Paule Vézelay, *Duet*, 1963, roller-printed cotton, Estate of Paule Vézelay

41
Paule Vézelay, *Modulation*, 1963, roller-printed cotton, Estate of Paule Vézelay

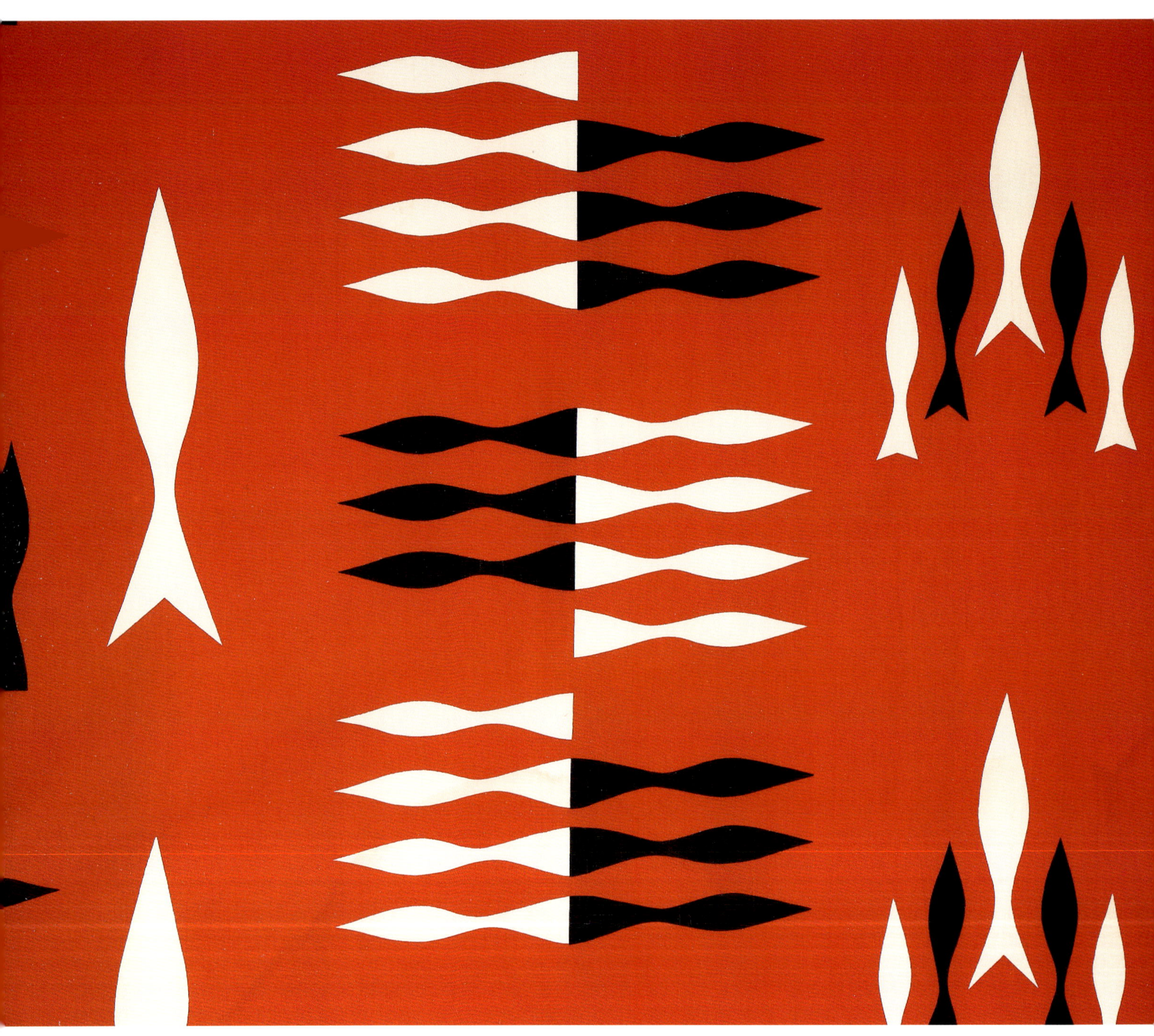

42
Paule Vézelay, *Elation*, 1957, roller-printed cotton,
Estate of Paule Vézelay

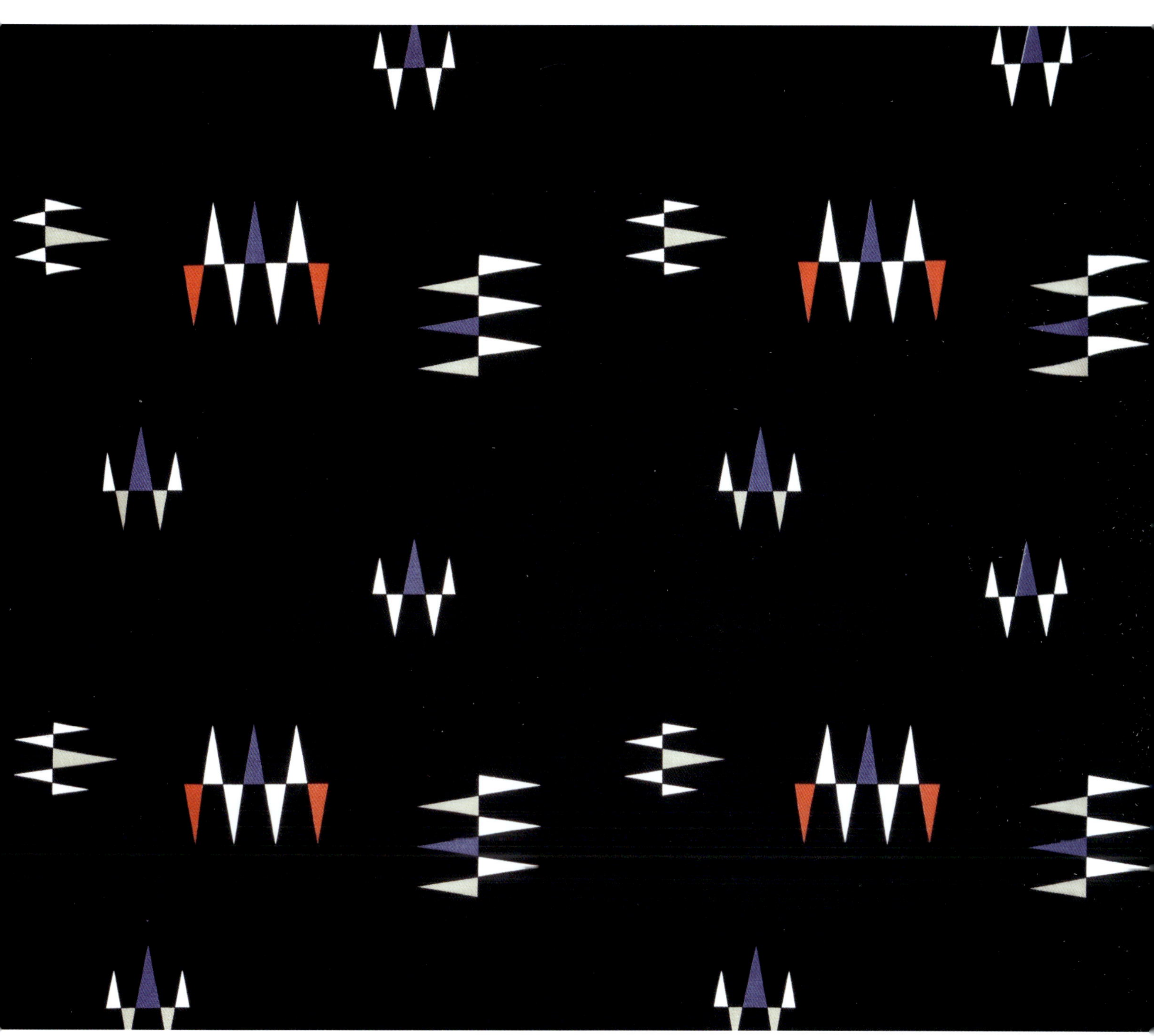

43
Paule Vézelay, *Pennons*, 1957, roller-printed cotton,
Estate of Paule Vézelay

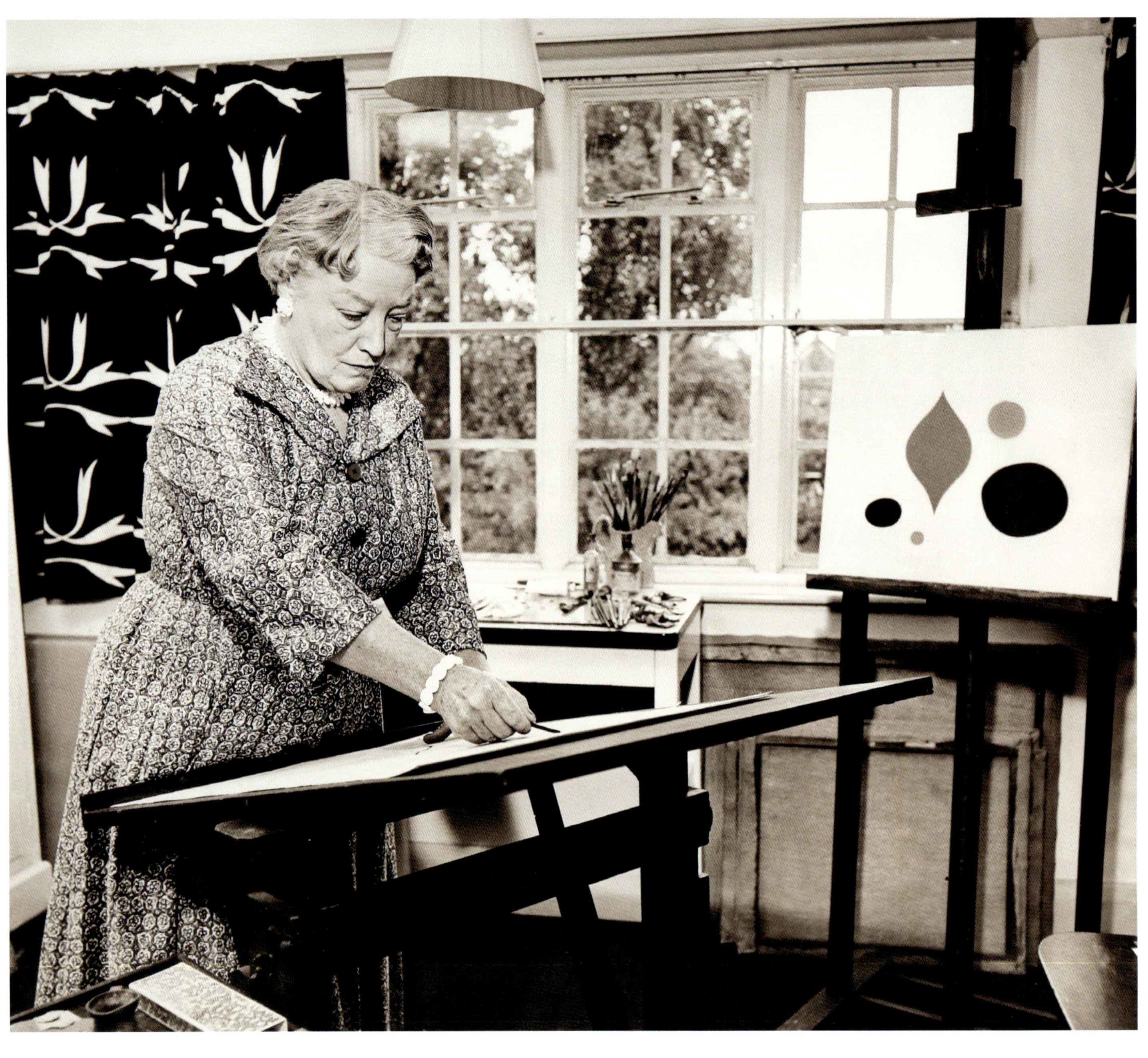

44
Paule Vézelay in her London studio with her 1955 textile *Harmony* (left) and her 1956 painting *The Yellow Circle* (right), photograph, Estate of Paule Vézelay

45
Paule Vézelay, *Stanza*, 1958, roller-printed cotton, Estate of Paule Vézelay

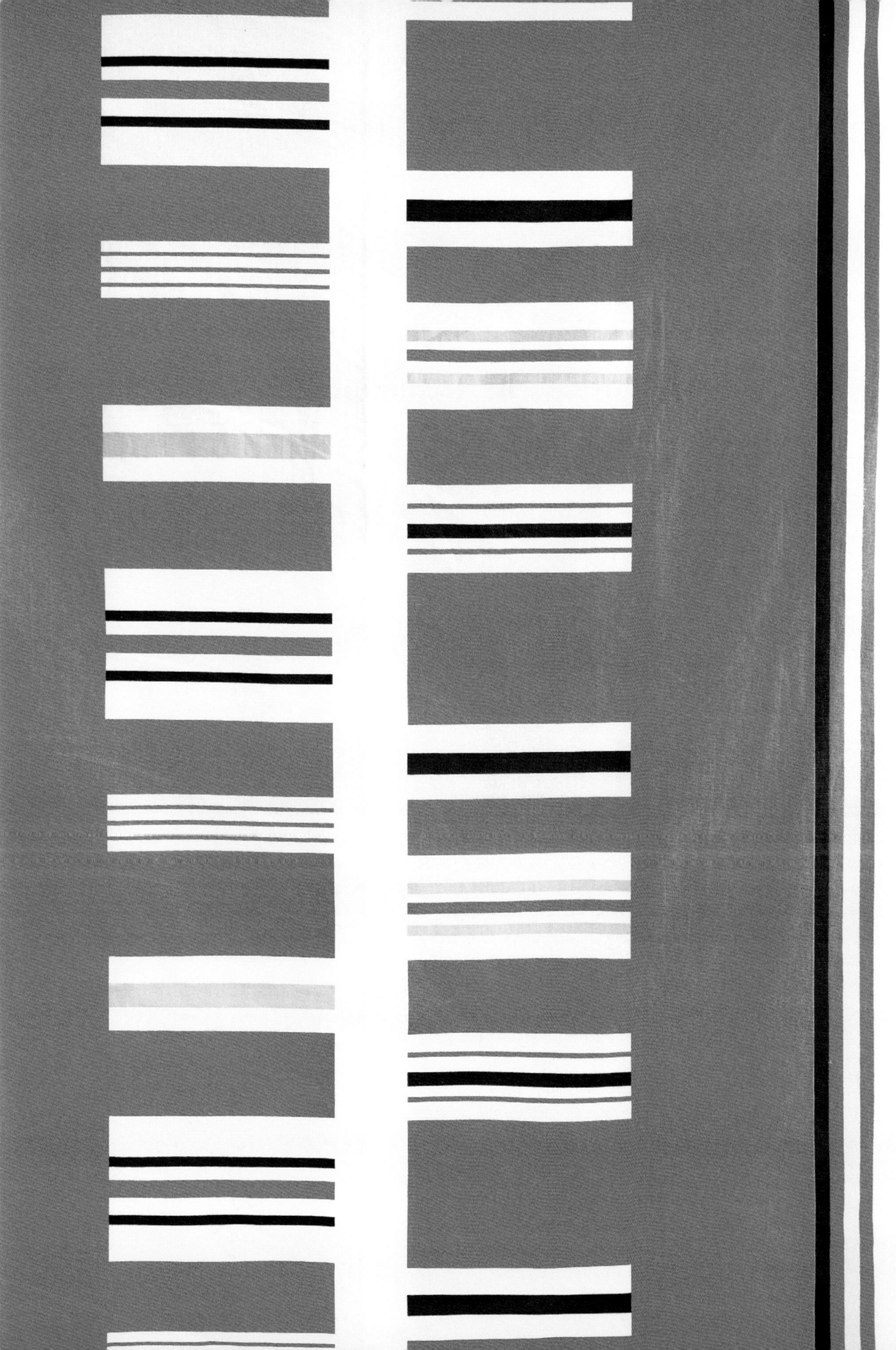

It is significant that, from the outset, Vézelay's textiles were singled out for exhibitions, journals and Heal's brochures. While the contemporaneous designs of Day, Brown and Jacqueline Groag, for example, are unmistakably in the period's Contemporary Style, Vézelay was aware that her designs were not. As she said to Germaine Greer, 'A painting or a drawing wants to have air indicated . . . I think a great many artists cram all kinds of forms and lines in their paintings which would be much better with half the number.'[26]

While it is possible to trace some motifs in Vézelay's textile designs back to her fine art, they are mostly original, demonstrating her outstanding ability to respond appropriately to every medium. Just as her prints, sculptures, drawings and *Lines in Space* are distinct from her paintings and from each other, so are her fabrics. At the same time, they share with her fine art a mastery of space through a play of two and three dimensions, elegance and restraint, mysterious forms, and intriguing juxtapositions of unusual colour tones, sustaining interest.

> *Perhaps we may think that the non-figurative textile designer has entered an exciting country . . . Designs of dignity and harmony need not lack that spirit of freedom which makes them authentically contemporary; the best among these designs already have their place with other fine productions in this country, and they will be recognised eventually as the treasured 'period pieces' of an epoch which is making a rich contribution to the art of design.*[27]

Thus, Vézelay, as early as 1959, correctly assessed her own place in textile history.

This chapter is based on original research conducted in 2018 for a longer essay submitted in support of the Courtauld Institute of Art Graduate Diploma in the History of Art in 2018 and the author's catalogue raisonné of extant textile samples.

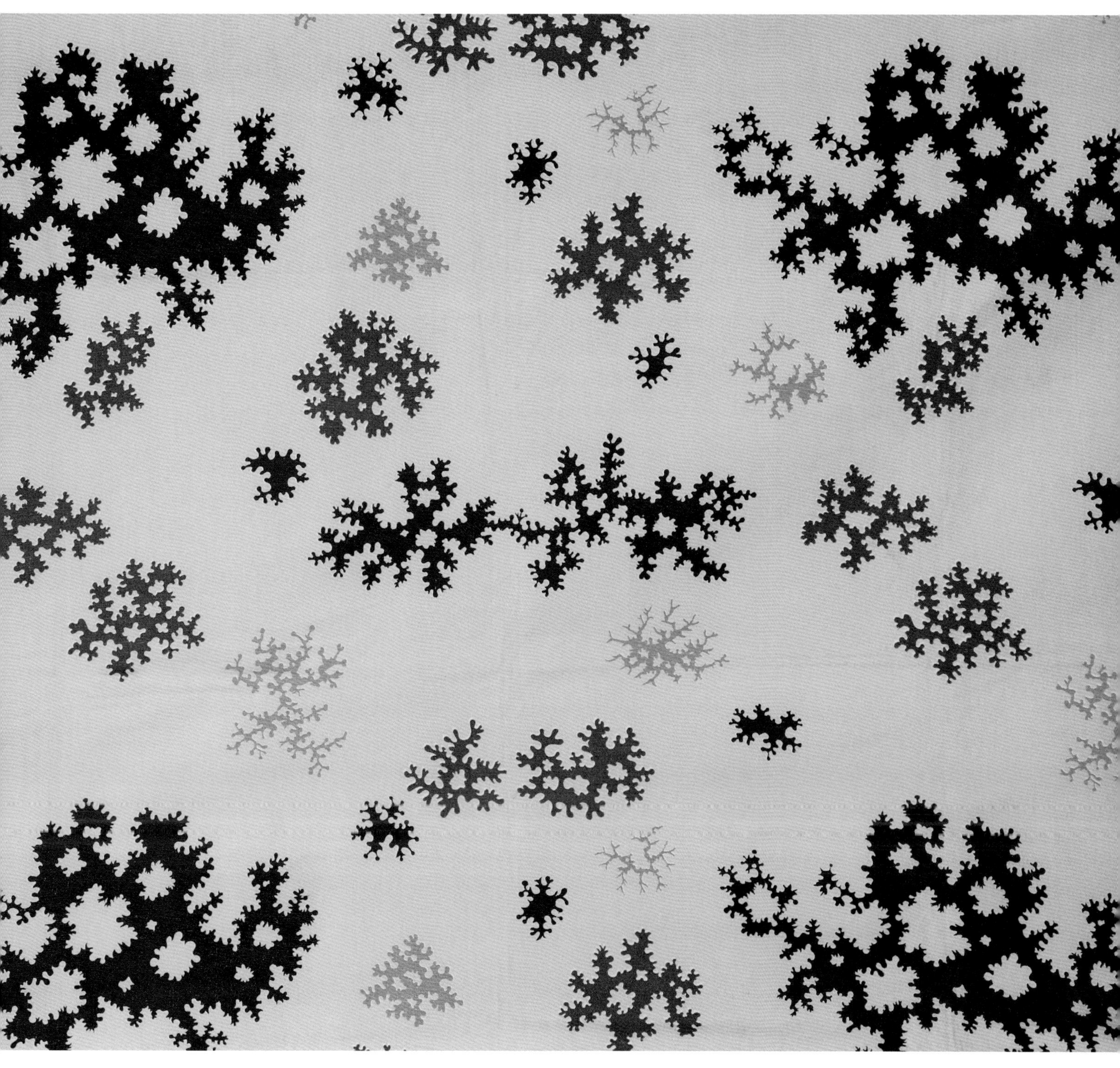

46
Paule Vézelay, *Froth*, 1960, roller-printed cotton,
Estate of Paule Vézelay

47
Paule Vézelay, *Eight Forms and Three Circles*, 1959, oil on canvas, 73 × 116 cm, Tate

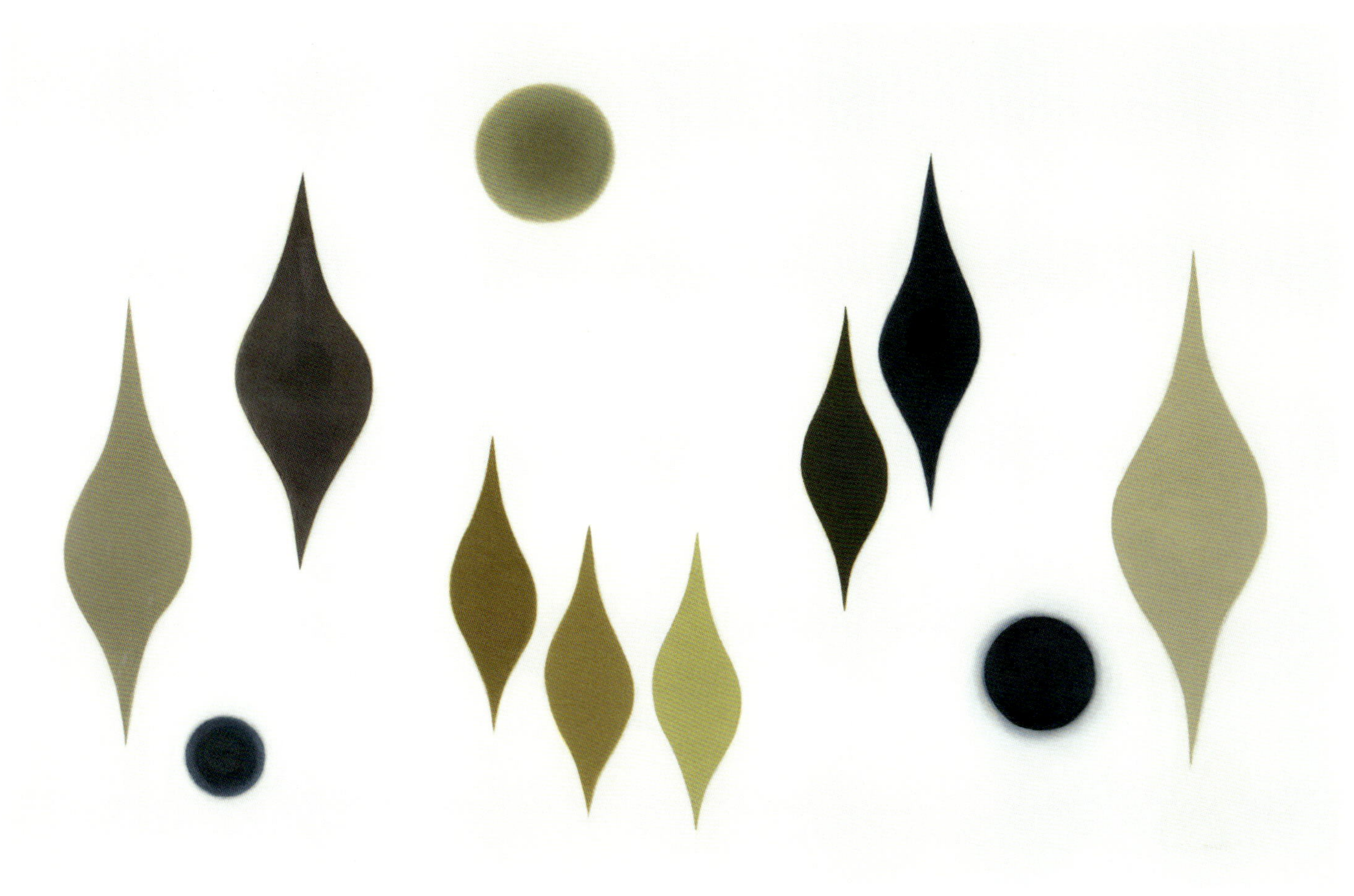

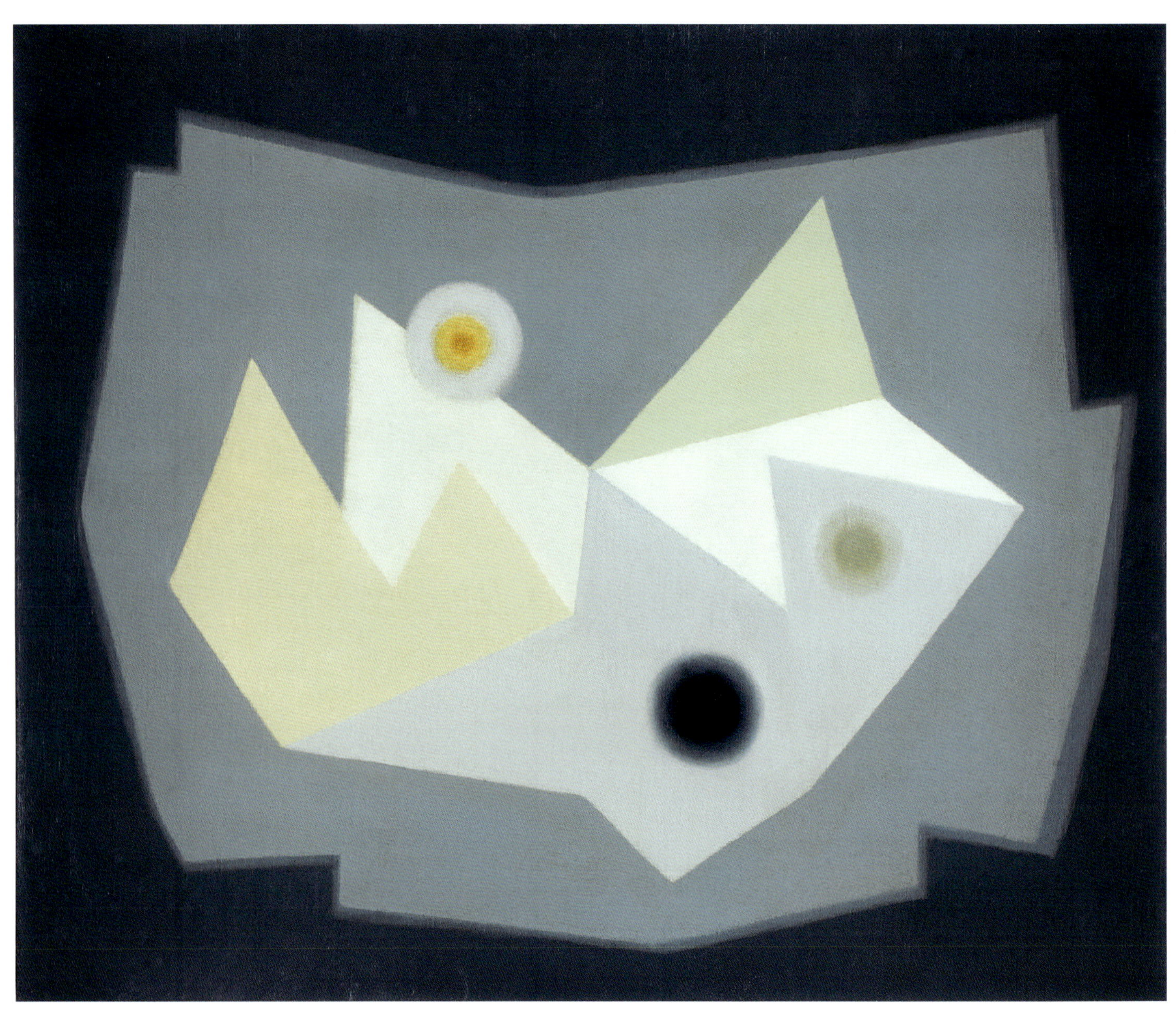

48
Paule Vézelay, *Grey and Yellow*, 1953,
oil on canvas, 64 × 53 cm, Pallant House Gallery,
Chichester

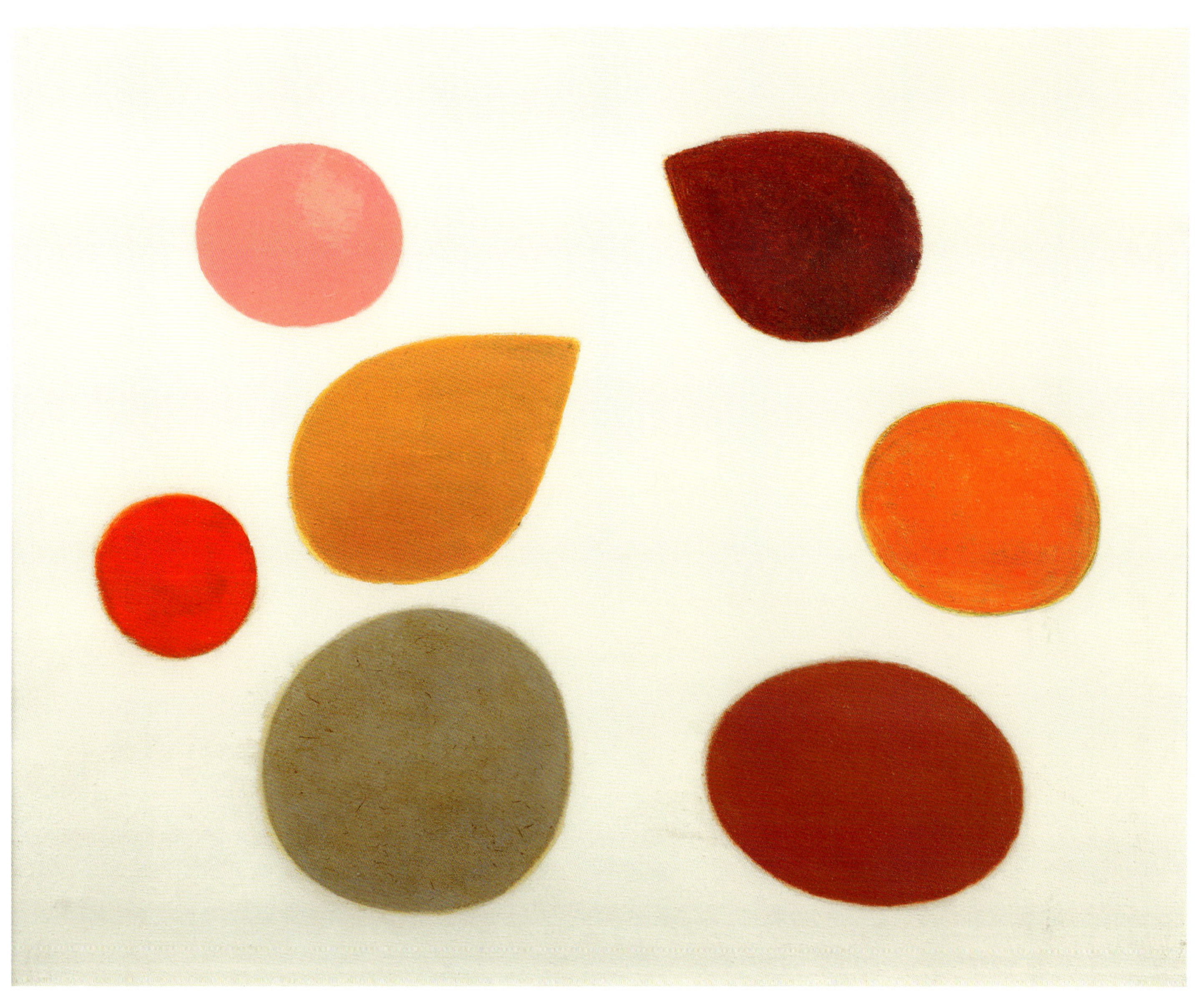

49
Paule Vézelay, *Seven Forms on White*, 1963,
oil on canvas, 50 × 62 cm, Estate of Paule Vézelay

50
Paule Vézelay, *Construction No.43: Four Silhouettes*, 1964, oil on board, relief, with one copper line and 15 parallel lines of thread, 66 × 35 cm, private collection

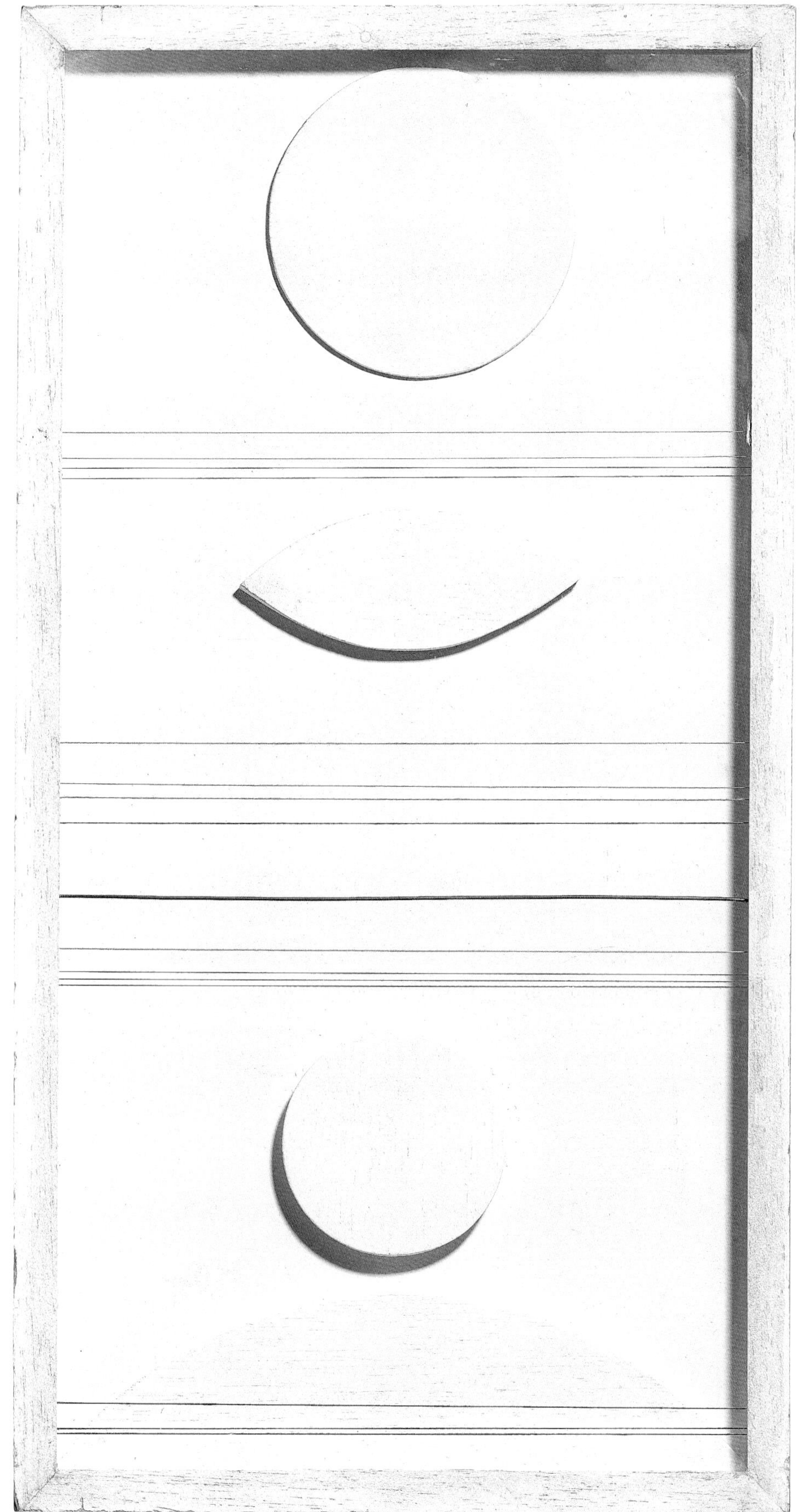

51
Paule Vézelay, *Two Red Forms*, 1968, oil and mixed media on canvas, 76 × 119 cm, private collection

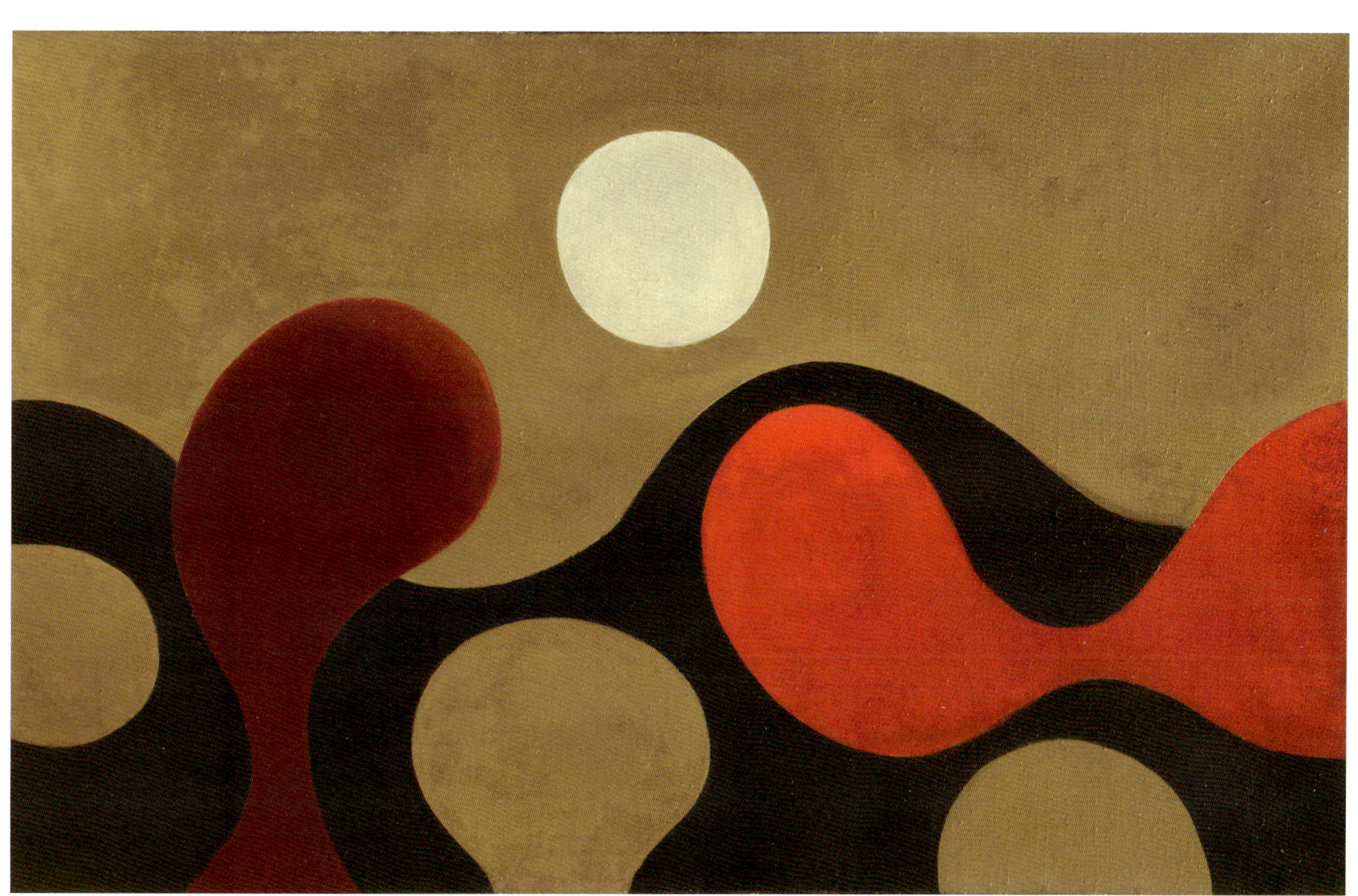

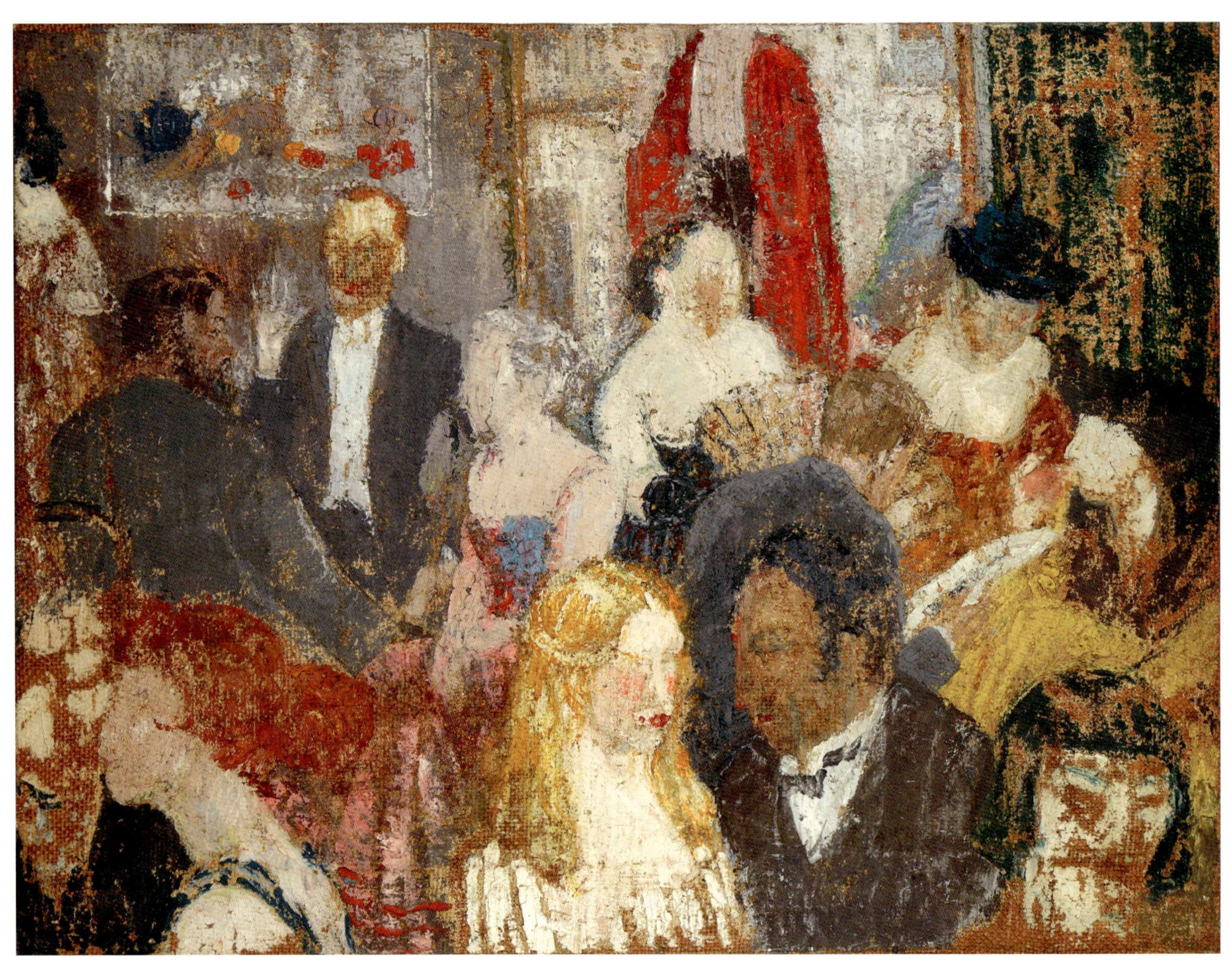

52
Marjorie Watson-Williams / Paule Vézelay,
Impressions of an Evening Party, c.1918,
oil on hessian, 20 × 24 cm, Estate of Paule Vézelay

Decades of Self-Reinvention

The seven productive decades of Paule Vézelay's career demanded not only stylistic evolutions but self-fashioning, self-reinvention, linked with place, time and remarkable encounters. By 1980, the moment of her first show in New York at the Zabriskie Gallery, she wrote, 'May I make the suggestion that I am not presented as a very old female artist of 87 . . . I *am* the first English abstract artist (not the first female artist) to have made an international reputation: in fact my abstract works were made sometime before those of Henry Moore, Ben Nicholson, Hepworth . . .'[1] Vézelay's dancing world of taut lines and pure, abstract shapes has a timeless quality when seen at Tate Britain with her contemporaries and Jean Hélion, the French intermediary for a new London–Paris axis.[2]

Born in 1892 and aged 20 in 1912, Marjorie Watson-Williams witnessed the last fanfare of Edwardian London. By 1922, aged 30, she had exhibited in Paris and Brussels as well as London. By 1932, at 40, Paule Vézelay, survivor of an intense relationship with the Surrealist artist André Masson, was showing at the Salon des surindépendants, along with female friends. By 1942, aged 50 in wartime Bristol, she could relive the memories of the triumphant retrospective in 1937 of her abstract paintings and sculptures at the Galerie Jeanne Bucher-Myrbor, attended by the cream of the Parisian art world. By 1952, at 60, she was exhibiting again in Paris at important *salons* and the Galerie Colette Allendy, as well as holidaying in Ascona with Hans Arp. The hope and colour of the Festival of Britain (1951) was reflected in her textile designs for Heal's. By 1962, at 70, Vézelay was encountering the Pop era, and at some date lunched with artist Allen Jones, during one of director Norman Reid's deliberately 'mixed' lunches of British artists at the Tate Gallery.[3] By 1972, when she was 80, the Tate Gallery was showing Barnett Newman and conceptual art. By 1982, post-modernism reigned. While new developments in the art world may have been baffling, Vézelay's high modernist retrospective was in preparation, curated by Bristol-born Ronald Alley, an expert on the School of Paris.[4] After the retrospective in 1983, her oeuvre re-entered the art world and feminist discourse, thanks to Germaine Greer, who interviewed her for BBC Television in 1984.

Vézelay's trajectory through the century invites comparisons. She did not suffer a career tragically cut short like Sophie Taeuber-Arp, nor witness most of her life's work destroyed by bombs like her Parisian contemporary from London, Marlow Moss. Vézelay lacked the experience of working in stone and bronze like Barbara Hepworth, whose important commissions extended beyond post-war Britain. Fahrelnissa Zeid, moving in Paris's 1950s abstract circles, was wealthy and well-connected; vital personal support was offered to artists linked to celebrated male companions – Nadia Khodasevich to Fernand Léger, Françoise Gilot to Pablo Picasso, or Niki de Saint Phalle to Jean Tinguely.[5] Vézelay was alone.

To go back in time to Edwardian London: at first, in homage to James McNeill Whistler, her doctor's daughter surname became an MW monogram; fireworks spattered *Clifton Fair by Night* (1909).[6] Next, Walter Sickert's versions of Edgar Degas's theatrical scenes informed *In a Theatre* (1917) – white pages of music jumping out from the orchestra pit seem premonitory. Articles were signed 'M. Watson-Williams', replaced by 'P. Vézelay' in the 1940s: the artist to whom she referred was always a 'he'.

Wartime London saw soldiers in their thousands grouped to depart for the trenches of northern France. 'All the men I'd ever known, danced with, they were all killed in the First World War. All the students I'd met at the art school', Vézelay recalled.[7] Refugee artists arrived in town, exhibiting at the Royal Academy and nationally. The young artist, known for her Beardsley-inspired *Punch* illustrations and those for Samuel Pepys Junior's *Diary of the Great Warr* (1916) was attractive.[8] One of these refugees, the Belgian artist Léon de Smet, introduced her to his social circle, including John Galsworthy of *The Forsyte Saga* fame.[9] Marjorie Watson-Williams would find her portrait by de Smet reproduced on the cover of the February 1919 edition of *Colour Magazine*, produced especially for the League of Belgian Artists.[10] In a white blouse and black skirt with a long crimson cloak, her hair drawn back and with striking black eyebrows, she emits more than a hint of severity. Note the modernism of the Whistlerian white ground and bare Japanese prints, but also the silhouette portrait and Staffordshire pottery figures on the fireplace that link this work to her art-student life: this is surely her apartment, not his studio.[11]

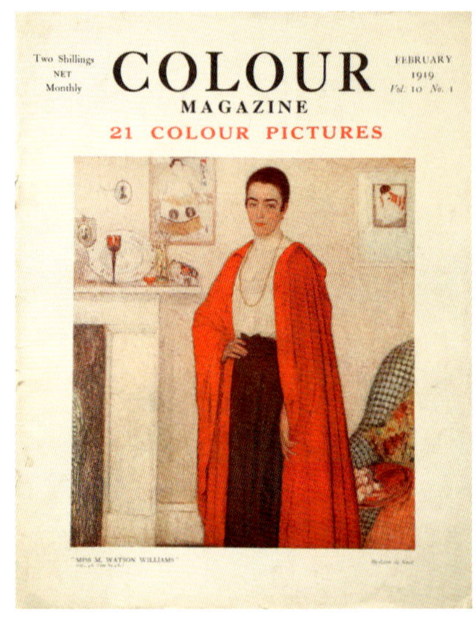

53
Cover illustration featuring *Portrait of Marjorie Watson-Williams* by Léon de Smet, *Colour Magazine*, vol.10, no.1, February 1919, Estate of Paule Vézelay

In a 1918 half-length portrait, a twinkling Venetian glass mirror above a cut-glass decanter in front of a Staffordshire plate serves as a foil for the sitter, whose jaunty hat on pinned-up hair provides a note of red.[12] The silhouette portrait, sharper here, again signals Vézelay's childhood fascination: 'I had first used cut silhouettes for book illustration, also using them as collages on charcoal; I had varied the tones of silhouettes in order to give them the illusion of a third dimension . . . I had made silhouettes in two and in three dimensions as an integral part of my constructions . . .'[13] The cut-out technique continued with her textile designs.

De Smet's *Femme nue allongée*, with the same dark hair undone, the sharp eyebrows and profile, the smooth extended back against decorative wallpaper, seems also to be Marjorie Watson-Williams.[14] We know she painted male nudes in George Belcher's studio when a student at the London School of Art. If indeed she posed nude for de Smet, this not only implied personal liberation but corroborates accounts of his pursuit and her desire to escape to Paris. She would have to create a modernist persona to accompany her art: her name would have to change.

Paris, a city constructed around historic monuments – Notre-Dame, the Louvre, the Invalides – traversed by a divided river, held three grandiose international exhibitions in the post-war years, all of which Paule Vézelay must have seen: Art Deco in 1925 (titled the *International Exposition of Modern Decorative and Industrial Arts and Modern Industries*), the Paris Colonial Exhibition of 1931, and the World Fair in 1937.[15] France's commitment to its post-Revolutionary and Enlightenment traditions embraced difference: Persia,

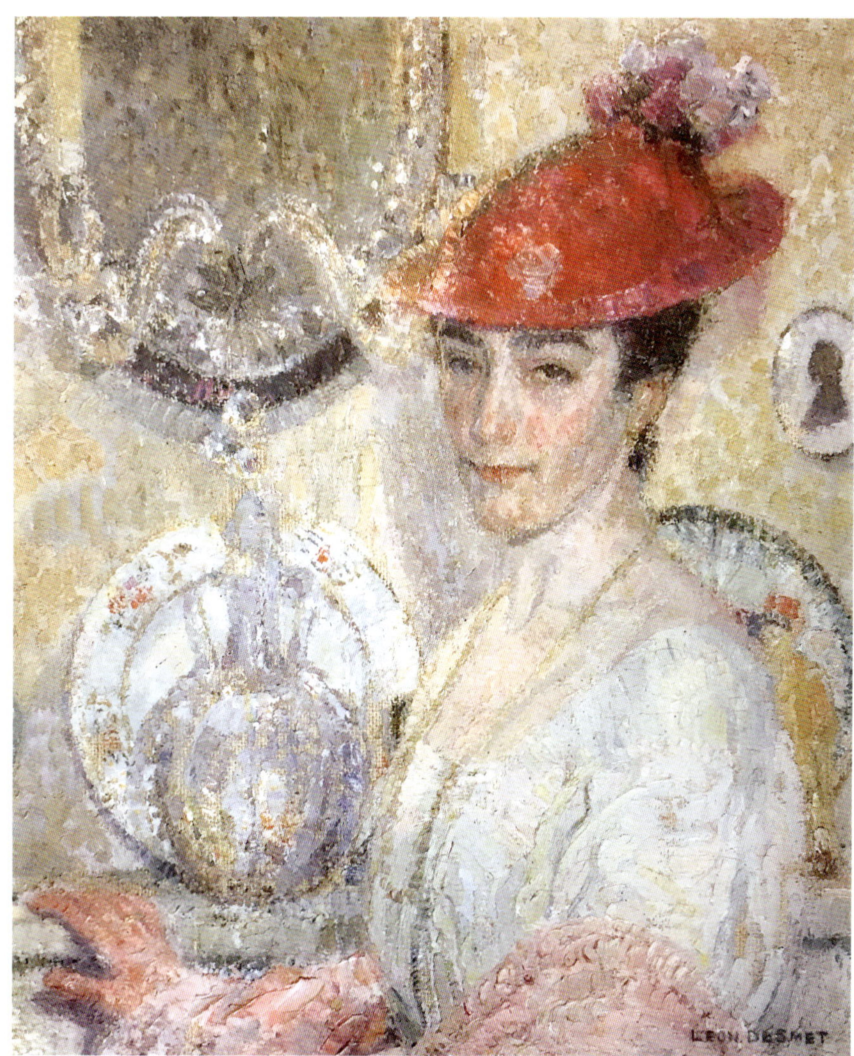

54
Léon de Smet, *Mlle Watson-Williams*, 1918, oil on canvas, 60 × 50 cm, private collection

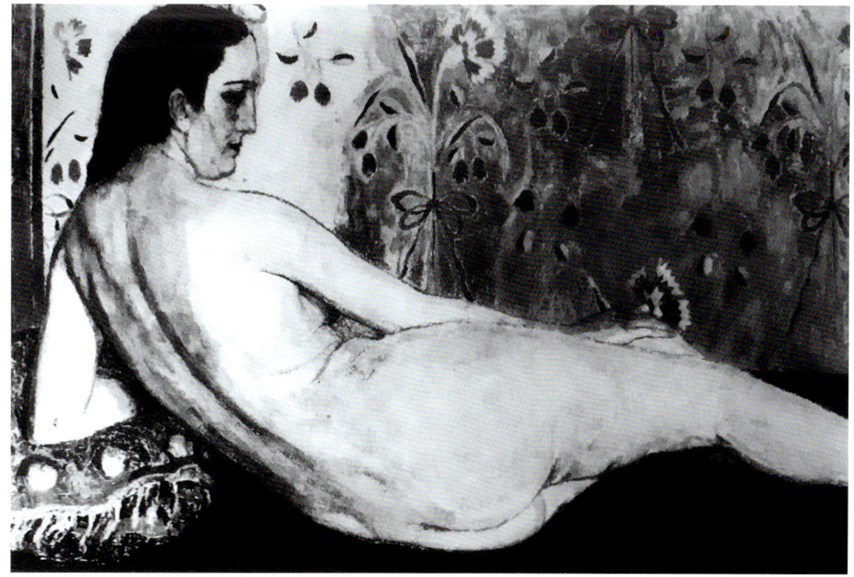

55
Léon de Smet, *Femme nue allongée*, c.1918, oil on canvas, location unknown

Asia, North Africa and Oceania, coinciding with its expansionist interests and expanded artistic styles. France dominated Europe, intellectually and artistically, until 1939.

Yet jazz-age Paris was a city whose cosmopolitanism was predicated upon war loss and imported labour; France's *industries de luxe* – food, wine, fashion, art and love – contrasted with grimy and monarchical London, with its reeking pubs. Edward VII may have confirmed the taste for Parisian escapades, but the sexual liberation of English women was more challenging. Living in Paris as a female artist implied a small private income, while *immigrées* from Eastern Europe became artists' models, mistresses or prostitutes. British girls, classless in Paris, had the vote (like the *américaines*), generating a self-worth that contrasted with their French counterparts, socially coded within a Catholic and highly stratified society.

Settling in Paris in 1926, Paule Vézelay took her surname from the hilltop town dominated by a Romanesque abbey; 'Paule' was as necessary as 'Claude' for the Surrealist photographer Claude Cahun (born Lucy Schwob). Marlow Moss (born Marjorie Jewell in London) had affected a similar self-reinvention, as a disciple of the abstract artist Piet Mondrian, and adopted a 'manly' appearance.[16] Sapphic Paris extended from Renée Vivien to Nathalie Clifford Barney or artist Romaine Brooks.[17] Polyamorous *amazones* proliferated: the Duchesse de la Salle in riding gear painted by Tamara de Lempicka in 1925 contrasted with a host of *garçonnes* in flapper mode. Yet Vézelay destroyed her painting *Deux femmes nues* (1927–8; fig.58) of two girls dancing. Abandoning the circus motifs, heavy bodies, and sailor and zig-zag motifs associated with Gustave de Smet, Léon's brother, she adopted Surrealism as a new terrain.

André Masson, her great love, was excluded from her Tate biography. Following a glorious holiday in 1930, the couple intended to marry. However Vézelay ended their increasingly turbulent relationship in 1932. Masson, illustrator of the Marquis de Sade's *Justine* and Georges Bataille's pornographic *Histoire de l'oeil* in 1928, was mentor to both her body and mind. How could such initiations and practices, imagined or experienced, be banished from Vézelay's life and writing – as though so many discoveries had never existed? Masson's inspiration affected Vézelay's drawing and painting, from calligraphic jagged lines to *personnages*, horse-like heads, inky contours and sandy grounds – her versions always more delicate, more whimsical.[18] Yet who is the praying mantis inside Alberto Giacometti's *Cage* of 1931, the year life became intolerable with her lover?[19] Vézelay was fascinated by a trope to which she returns: the praying mantis, who devours her mate during copulation.[20]

Vézelay moved to the Abstraction-Création circle, creating the white plaster biomorphic sculptures and *jardinières* by 1935. She became ever closer to the ex-Dada painter, sculptor and poet Arp and his artist wife, Sophie Taeuber-Arp. Vézelay's innovative *Lines in Space* recall his handmade, box-like frames, sheltering painted wood reliefs, where shadow-play doubles the curves of biomorphic shapes. As a trio they exhibited and holidayed together in 1939. Vézelay's best post-war writing is a tribute to Sophie, who died, tragically asphyxiated, in 1943.[21]

With the start of the war, it was the unmarried daughter who returned to Bristol to care for her mother (her famous father having died in late 1938). With a permit from Sir Kenneth Clark, she depicted bomb damage like any John

56
Marlow Moss, photograph by Stephen Storm, Nijhoff I Oosthoek Collection, Zurich

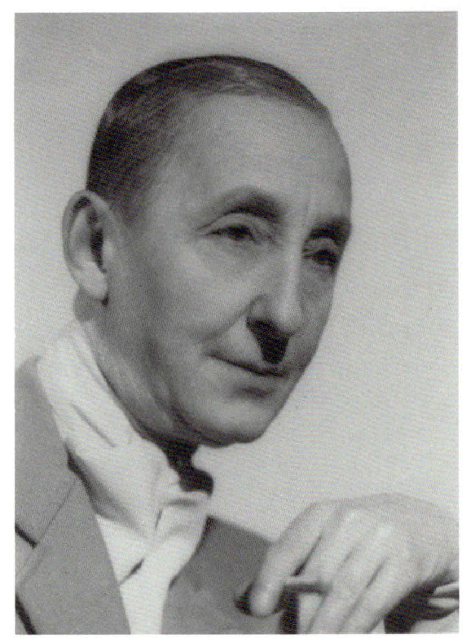

57
Marlow Moss, *White and Yellow)*, 1935, oil paint, string and canvas on canvas, 77.6 × 55 cm, Tate

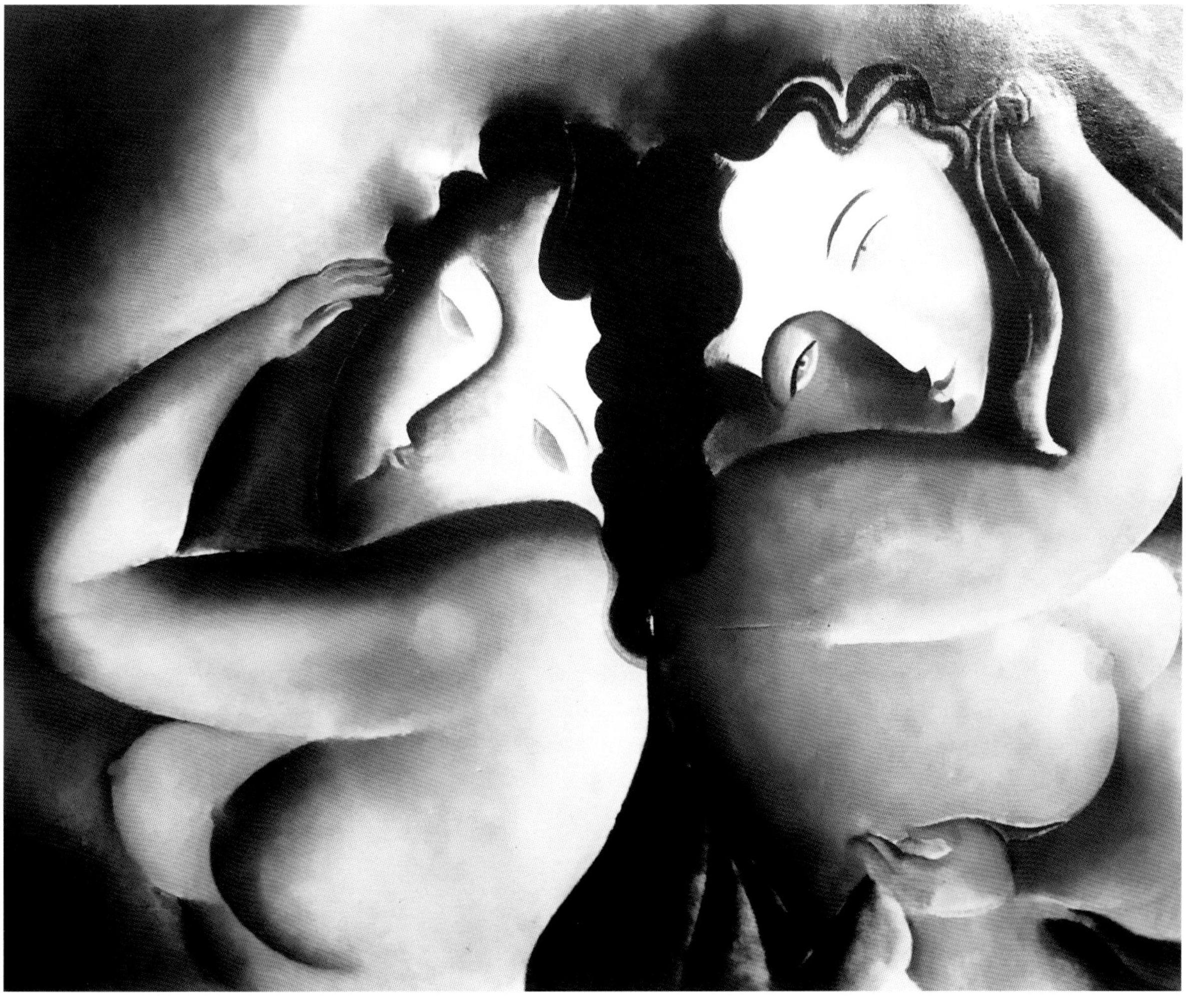

58
Paule Vézelay, *Deux femmes nues*, 1927–8, oil on canvas (destroyed by artist)

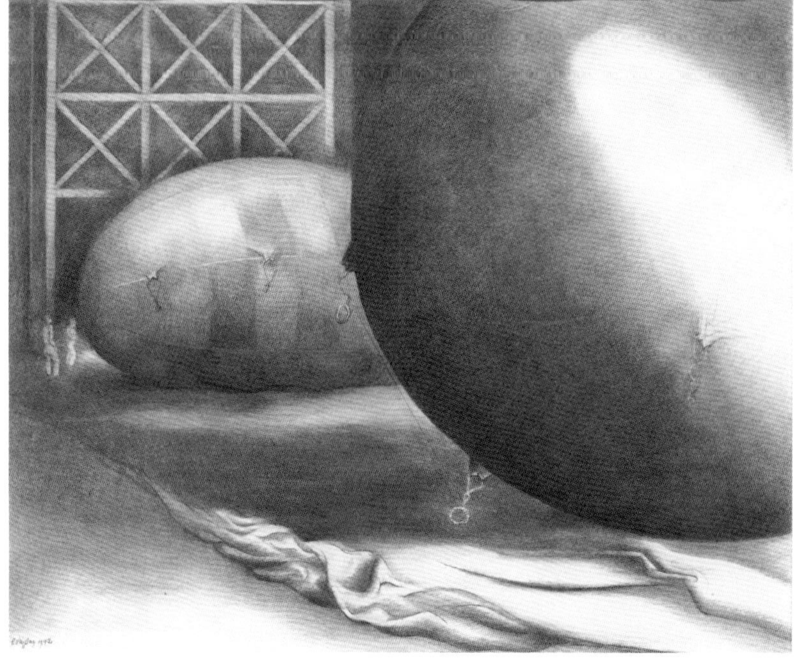

59
Paule Vézelay, *Barrage Balloon at a Balloon Centre*, 1942, Tate Archive

Piper or Graham Sutherland, moving to the terrain of the barrage balloons, 'managed by teams of women in uniform: tough monsters coming to life', as she recalled for the BBC.[22]

Thrilled to rediscover Paris after the war, Vézelay was reborn. She had another solo show with Jeanne Bucher in 1946, whose death later that year from cancer, alas, spelled the end of her hospitality. Colette Allendy, widow of the famous psychoanalyst Dr René Allendy, had a small gallery in the 16th arrondissement. There, Vézelay staged another retrospective in late 1946 – to be followed by artists such as Francis Picabia.[23]

An exchange of poems with Arp continued into the 1940s. She refused Arp's hand in marriage: living with him in Ascona would involve unwelcome domestic labour.[24] His *Fabliaux sombres* poem, with Battle of Hastings images, arrived too late for her Saint George's Gallery show in 1949.[25] In a still prudish present, surely the 1950s, she wrote 'Chastity', a text moving awkwardly from Etruscan phallus worship to the plight of the unmarried mother.[26] Arp died in 1966: there would be no more sharing of memories in French of the Paris where a certain Paule Vézelay had come to life.

At 74, the single gentlewoman living in Barnes was the only persona that remained, surrounded by her paintings, sculptures and beloved Staffordshire pottery.[27] She was still creative, although – *The Lazy Artist*, a poem of 1969, is regressively Wordsworthian.[28] Other dated typescripts show her desire to write theoretical texts and give illustrated talks. A manuscript of 1970 was accepted by the multidisciplinary journal *Leonardo*.[29] In 1973 she gifted the splendid and delicate *Construction. Grey Lines on Pink Ground* (1938; fig.13) to the Tate – entailing curators' visits, conversations and correspondence.[30]

One imagines Paule Vézelay at her Tate Gallery retrospective of 1983: memories of Paris mingling with present satisfactions; seeing the colour and movement of her lines and shapes in space, the white dynamism of her sculptural forms. Her interview with Germaine Greer preserves her exceptional style on screen: the long white bob and black dress, the 1930s Art Deco necklace, her decorum and twinkling humour on camera. Greer shows surprising tact as she mentions Masson, Arp, competitors, her own book on female artists, even happiness – 'I dislike sad art', says Vézelay.[31] It is an extraordinary encounter between generations.

Vézelay transcended her multiple pasts with persistent self-belief. The purity of her commitment to her art – impeded by the 'obstacle race' (Greer's phrase) – linked to 20th-century credos and canons, was and is exemplary.

60
André Masson, *La Corde*, 1924, oil on canvas, 45.1 × 38.2 cm, Scottish National Gallery of Modern Art, Edinburgh

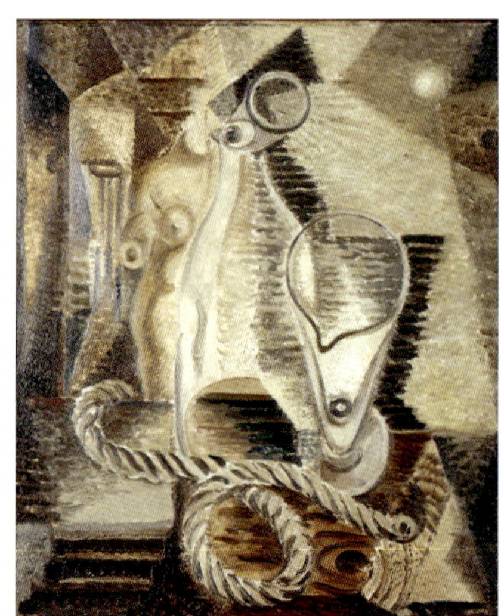

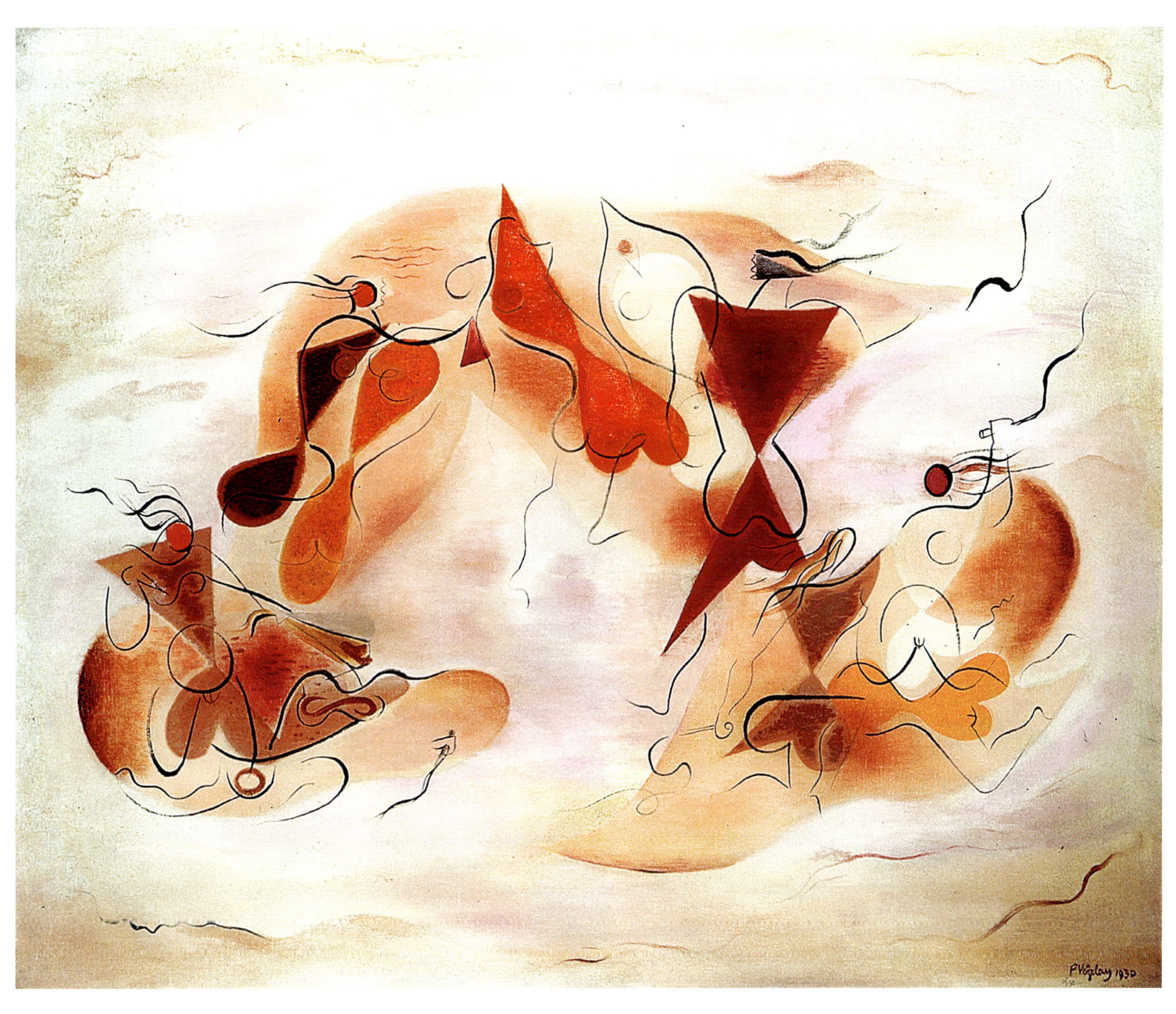

61
Paule Vézelay, *The Storm, Women Fighting*, 1930,
oil on canvas, 81 × 100 cm, private collection

62
Paule Vézelay, *Youth Leaving Old Age*, 1934, oil on canvas, 73.6 × 81.3 cm, Estate of Paule Vézelay

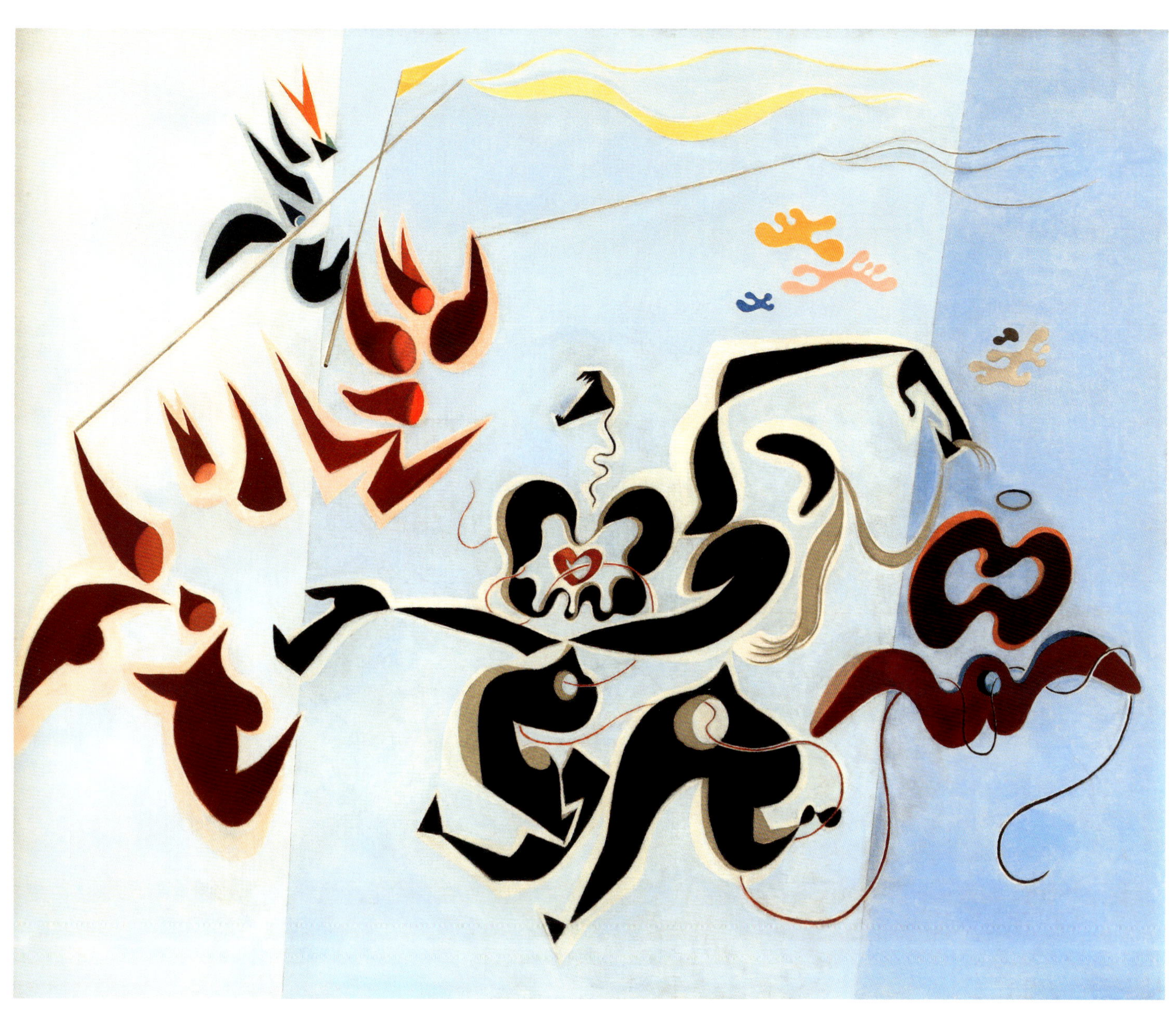

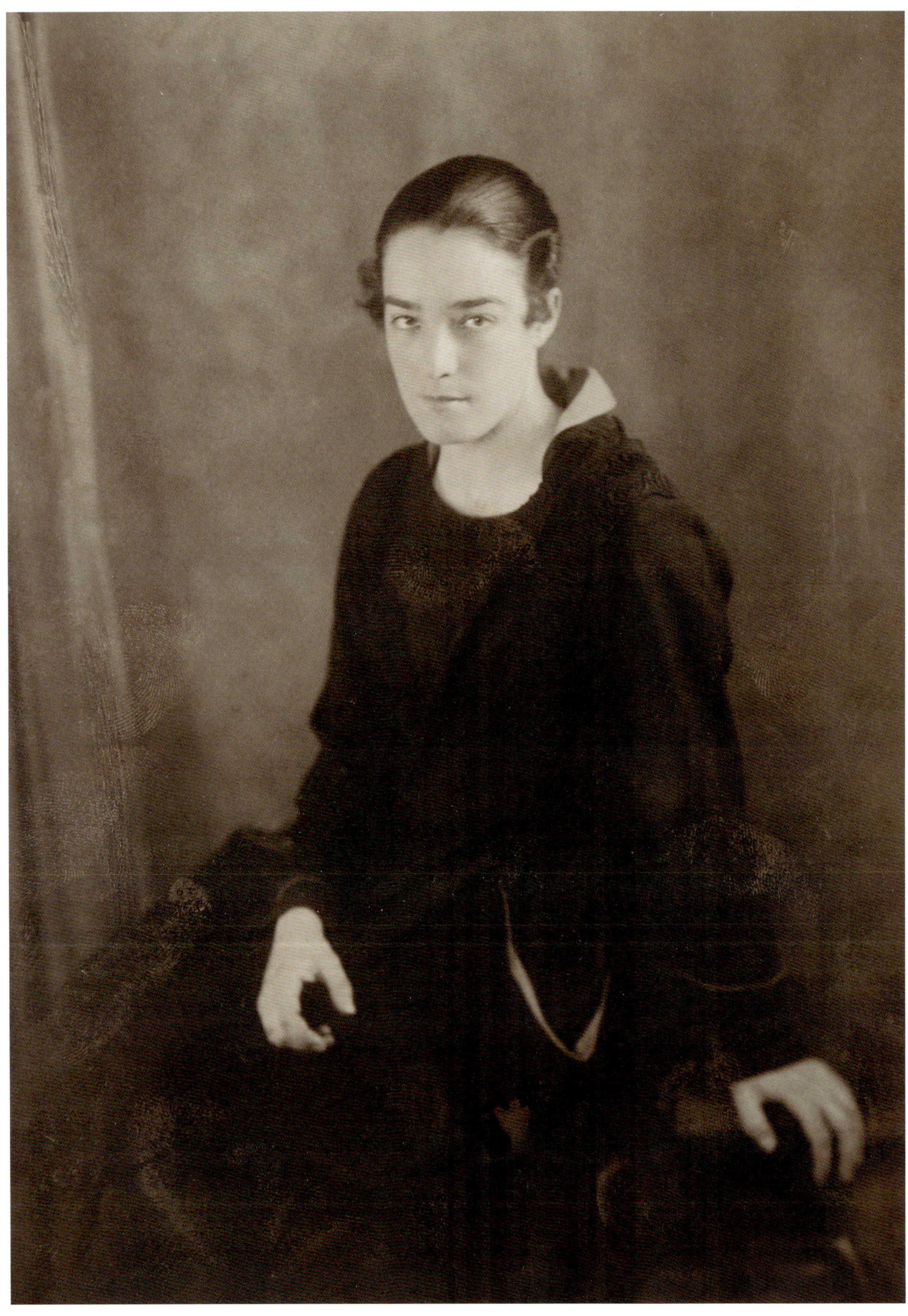

63 Marjorie Watson-Williams / Paule Vézelay, Paris, early 1920s, photograph by Paul Delbo, Estate of Paule Vézelay

Illustrated Chronology

Compiled by Nina Gioria

1892
Born Marjorie Agnes Watson-Williams, 14 May, in Clifton, Bristol. Grew up in a family of two brothers, Eric and Guthrie, sister Ruth and step-sister Marjorie. Her mother, Margaret, assisted Belgian refugees during the First World War. Her father, Patrick, was an ear, nose and throat doctor and amateur artist.

1909–12
Studied painting and etching at the Bristol School of Art.

1912–14
Moved to London to study at the Slade School of Fine Art but soon transferred to the London School of Art, where she was taught by John Hassall and became head of George Belcher's class. Also attended evening classes in lithography at Chelsea Polytechnic.

1916
Illustrated *A Diary of the Great Warr* by 'Saml. Pepys Jnr', published by John Lane.

1917–18
Met the Belgian artist Léon de Smet.
Wrote and illustrated articles on London life for *Drawing and Design* magazine.

1918
Exhibited at the New English Art Club, the Senefelder Club and the Society of Wood Engravers.

1920
Joint exhibition, *Exhibition of Oil Paintings & Lithographs by Léon de Smet and Charcoal Drawings, Pastels, Lithographs and Watercolours by M. Watson-Williams*, Finnigans, Deansgate, Manchester.
Joint exhibition, *M. Watson-Williams & Gustave de Smet*, Galerie Georges Giroux, Brussels.
First visit to Cirque Medrano, Paris.
First solo exhibition, *M. Watson-Williams*, Galerie des Feuilles d'Art, Paris.

1921
Solo exhibition, *M. Watson-Williams*, Dorien Leigh Galleries, London.
Exhibited at Salon de la Société Nationale des Beaux Arts, Paris.

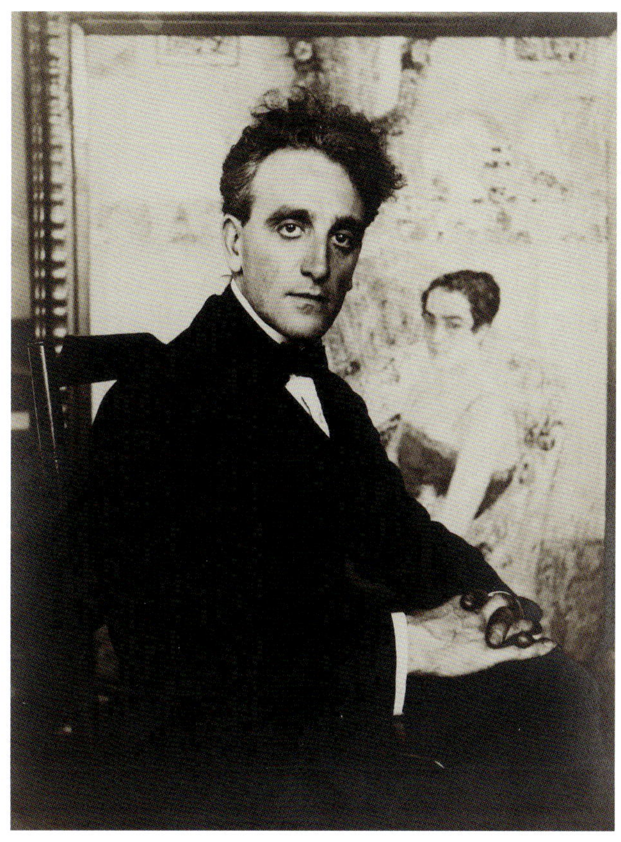

64
Léon de Smet in front of his portrait of Marjorie Watson-Williams, c.1920, photograph, Estate of Paule Vézelay

1922
Became a member of the London Group (until 1933).
Spent six months in Austria.

1923–4
First visit with Margaret Morris and J.D. Fergusson to Cap d'Antibes with Morris's summer dance school.
Exhibited in the British pavilion, Venice Biennale.

1924
Solo exhibition, *Marjorie Watson-Williams, Peintre*, Galerie Louis Manteau, Brussels.
Exhibited in *The English Society of Wood-Engravers*, Art Institute of Chicago.

1925
Second visit to Margaret Morris's summer school at Cap d'Antibes.
Solo exhibition, *M. Watson-Williams*, Château des Enfants, Cap d'Antibes, France.
Organised the exhibition *Pictures, Sculpture and Pottery by Some British Artists of Today*, Lefevre Galleries, London.

1926
Settled in Paris, moving to 7 Rue de la Grande Chaumière, Montparnasse.

1927
Changed her name to Paule Vézelay.
Exhibited in the Salon d'Automne in the Grand Palais, Paris.
Gallerist Jeanne Bucher made her first visit to Paule Vézelay's studio.

1928
Made her first abstract work (a drawing now lost).
Solo exhibition, *Paule Vézelay*, at the Galerie Alice Manteau, Paris.
Solo exhibition, *Paule Vézelay: Painting and Drawings*, Alex Reid & Lefevre Ltd (Lefevre Galleries), London.

1929
Became a member of the Salon des surindépendants, exhibiting yearly there until 1937.
Started a relationship with French artist André Masson and lived with him until 1932.

1930
Solo exhibition, *Paule Vézelay*, Galerie Vavin-Raspail, Paris. Catalogue preface by the French Surrealist poet Robert Desnos.
Exhibited in group exhibition *De Onafhankelijken* at the Stedelijk Museum, Amsterdam.

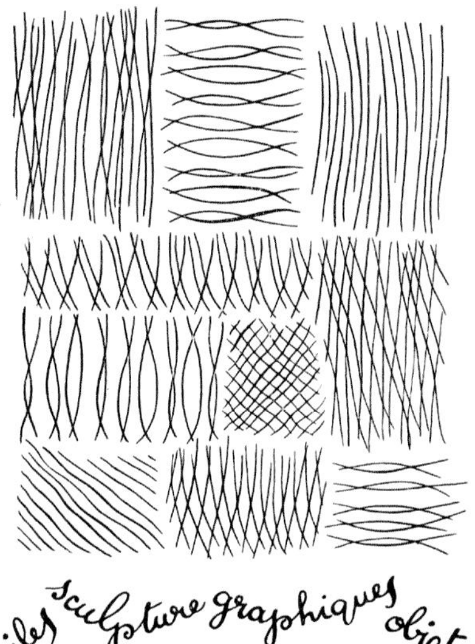

65
Exhibition card for Paule Vézelay's exhibition at Galerie Jeanne Bucher-Myrbor, 1937, Estate of Paule Vézelay

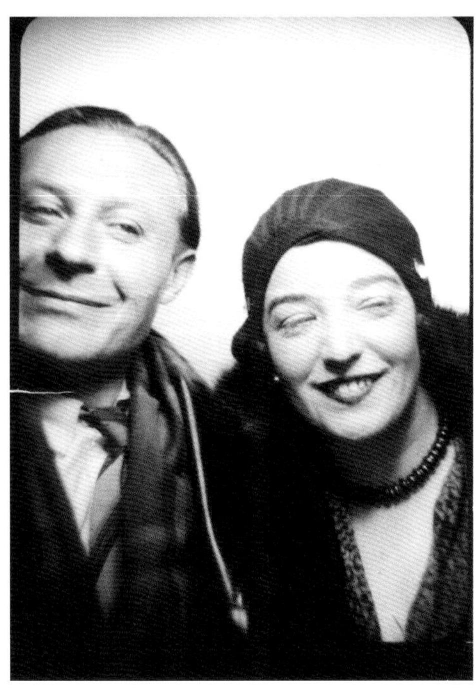

66
Photobooth picture of André Masson and Paule Vézelay, c.1930, 12.6 × 17.7 cm, Tate Archive

abstraction
création
art non
figuratif 1934

albers	page	3
arp		2
beothy		4
bill		5
brencusi		6
buchholster		9
calder		8
closon		7
conne		9
delaunay		10
domela-nieuwenhuis		12
dreier		11
eltzbacher		11
erni		13
fernandez		15
fischli		17
freundlich		14
gercin		10
gleizes		18
gonzales		16
gorin		20
gorky		19
hanser		22
hélion		24
herbin		21
hepworth		23
hone		27
huf		25
jelinek		26
jellett		24
kandinsky		29
kann		39
kosnick-kloss		27
kupka		28
moholy-nagy		31
mondrian		32
moss		30
nicholson		35
okamoto		33
paalen		37
power		34
prampolini		36
reth		39
roubillotte		38
schiess		42
schwitters		40
schoop		43
séligmann		41
taeuber-arp		19
tihanyi		43
van doesburg		46
vantongerloo		44
valmier		50
vargas		47
vézelay		48
villeri		51
vordemberge-gildewart		45
vulliemy		48

3

prix .. 15 francs
étranger 20 francs

67
Cover of *Abstraction-Création*, no.3, 1934,
Estate of Paule Vézelay

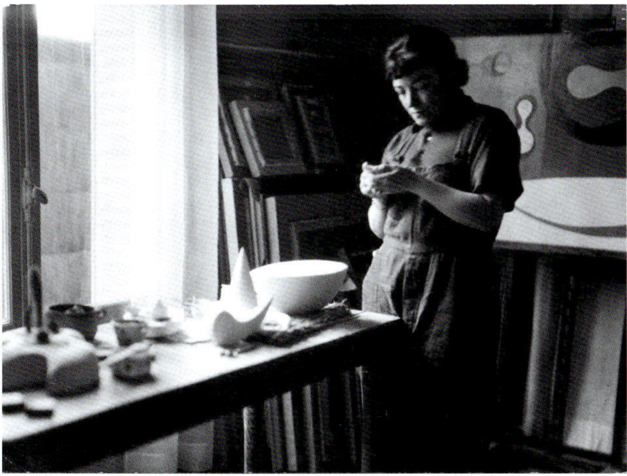

68
Paule Vézelay in her Paris studio, 1935,
photograph by Hugo P. Herdeg, Tate Archive

1932–3

Exhibited in group exhibition, *Confédération des artistes d'avant-garde, Paris–Tokio*, Tokyo. Exhibition toured to Osaka, Kyoto, Fukuoka, Kanazawa and Nagoya.
Ended relationship with André Masson.

1933

Exhibited in the third Abstraction-Création exhibition, Paris.

1934

Elected a member of the Abstraction-Création group (until 1936).
After several months in London, returned to Paris in October to live at 23 Rue Bénard.
Solo exhibition, *Toiles récentes de Paule Vézelay*, Galerie Jeanne Bucher, Paris.
Around this time Vézelay met Sophie Taeuber-Arp and Jean Arp.

1935

Began her *Recherches en trois dimensions* with her first collages, leading to her first *Lines in Space* works.

1936

Solo exhibition, *Paule Vézelay: Painting and Sculptures*, Alex Reid & Lefevre Ltd (Lefevre Galleries), London.

1937

Solo exhibition: exhibited her *Lines in Space* constructions and plaster sculptures in *Paule Vézelay: toiles, sculptures, graphiques et objets*, Galerie Jeanne Bucher-Myrbor, Paris.

1938

Exhibited in *L'art concret à Milan: Arp, Domela, Kandinsky, Magnelli, Seligmann, Taeuber-Arp, Vézelay*, Galeria Il Milione, Milan.
Exhibited in *Internationale de l'art non-figuratif*, Gemeentemuseum, Amsterdam.
Exhibited in *Tentoonstelling Abstracte Kunst*, Stedelijk Museum, Amsterdam.
Travelled through Italy to Assisi, Pisa, Rome, Venice and Milan.
Exhibited in *Exhibition of Collages, Papiers-Collés, and Photomontages*, co-curated by Jean Arp, Guggenheim Jeune, London.

1939

Exhibited in *Réalités nouvelles*, Galerie Charpentier, Paris.
Returned to England one month after the beginning of the Second World War.

1939–44

Spent the early part of the war in Bristol, where she received a temporary war artist's permit from Sir Kenneth Clark to record the bomb damage in Bristol.

1940
Set up and ran the Women's Defence Corps in Bristol with help from the women's rights campaigner and MP for Frome, Mavis Tate.

1942
Solo exhibition, *Recent works by Paule Vézelay*, Alex Reid & Lefevre Ltd (Lefevre Galleries), London.

1943
13 January, death of Sophie Taeuber-Arp.

1944
Moved to London and settled permanently in England after 1946.
Became a member of the Artists' International Association (AIA) until 1947.

1946
Solo exhibition, *Paule Vézelay*, Galerie Jeanne Bucher, Paris.
Exhibited in Salon des réalités nouvelles, Paris (yearly until 1957).
Solo exhibition, *Paule Vézelay: Oeuvres de 1928 à 1946*, Galerie Colette Allendy, Paris.
1 November, death of Jeanne Bucher.

1948
Became a fellow of the Salon des réalités nouvelles.
Elected Member of the Society of Industrial Artists as a designer of printed textiles and illustrator (elected a Fellow in 1958).

1949
Solo exhibition, *Paule Vézelay: Moving and Static Forms*, St George's Gallery, London.

1950
Solo exhibition, *Paule Vézelay: Oeuvres récentes*, Galerie Colette Allendy, Paris.
Exhibited in *P. Vézelay, George Fairley, Alan Davie*, Gimpel Fils Gallery, London.

1953
Founded the British branch of the Groupe Espace, an association of Abstract artists and architects founded by André Bloc in Paris in October 1951.

1955
Organised the exhibition *Le Groupe Espace of Great Britain*, Royal Festival Hall, London.
Joint exhibition, *Paule Vézelay: Lines in Space and Their Shadows (1936–1954); & Winifred Nicholson: Recent Paintings*, Ernest Brown & Phillips Ltd, Leicester Galleries, London.

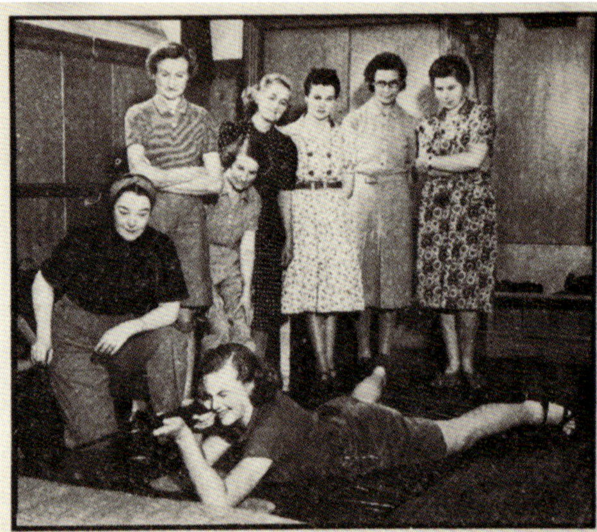
THEY AIM TO DEFEND.—Members of the newly-formed Bristol branch of the Women's Defence Corps at their first practice on the miniature range.

69
Paule Vézelay and the Bristol branch of the Women's Defence Corps, from the *Bristol Evening World & Evening Times & Echo*, 5 September 1940. Vézelay kneels on the left of the picture. Estate of Paule Vézelay

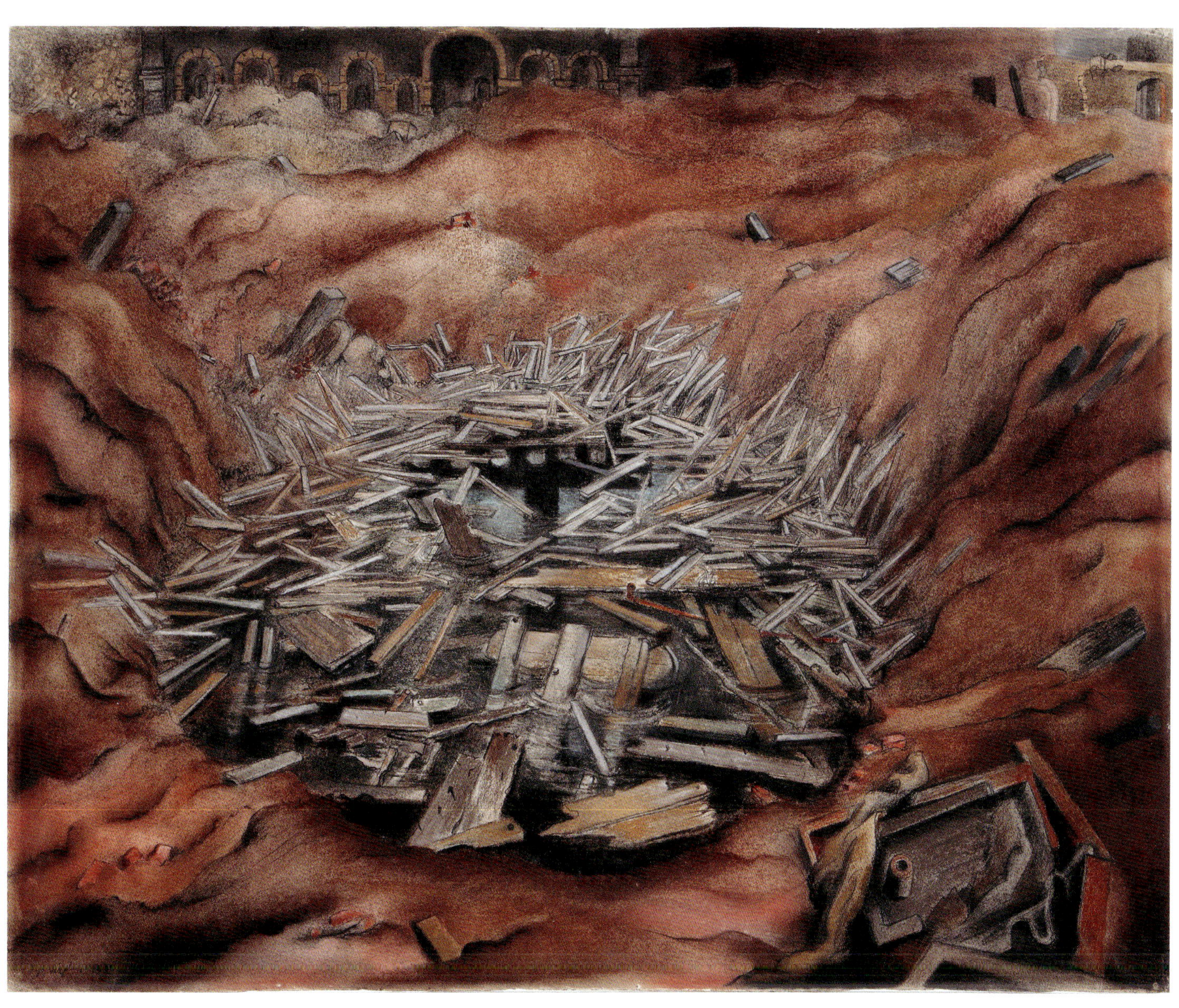

70 Paule Vézelay, *Bomb Damage in Bristol*, 1942, pastel, 59 × 74 cm, private collection

Groupe Espace

an international association of modern architects and non-figurative artists, was founded in Paris in 1951. Groupes have since been formed in Switzerland, Italy, and Sweden and, recently, by Madame Paule Vézelay in Great Britain.

The exhibition will include invited works by members of the Groupe Espace, Paris:
Jean Arp (France)
Etienne Beothy (France)
Soniá Delaunay (France)
Dr Walter Gropius (USA)
Day Schnabel (USA)
and paintings, sculpture, constructions in three dimensions, and architects' models, by members of the Groupe in Great Britain:
Vivien Pilley, FRIBA, MSIA
Jerzy Faczynski, Dip.Ing.Arch.
Bernard Carter
Geoffrey Clarke
Ithel Colquhoun
Bertram F. E. Eaton
Charles Howard
Marlow Moss
Vera Spencer
Paule Vézelay
and associate members

President of Honour:
M. René Varin, CBE,
Conseilleur Culturel près de l'Ambassade de France en Grande-Bretagne

First exhibition of the

Groupe Espace

of Great Britain

The Ceremonial Foyer, Royal Festival Hall,

London SE1

22 October—7 November inclusive

Private view Saturday 22 October 2-6 pm

The Ceremonial Foyer is open only to those attending concerts or ceremonies in the Festival Hall, but this card will admit two for the private view.

Groupe Espace

France

Italy

Switzerland

Sweden

Great Britain

71
Exhibition card for Groupe Espace at the Royal Festival Hall, London, 1955, Estate of Paule Vézelay

1957
Exhibited in *50 ans de peinture abstraite* at the Galerie Raymond Creuze, Paris.
Moved to Barnes, southwest London, where she lived until her death.

1964
Exhibited in the *London Group 1914–64, Jubilee Exhibition (Fifty Years of British Art)*, Tate Gallery, London.

1966
7 June, death of Jean Arp.

1968
Solo exhibition, *Paule Vézelay Retrospective: Drawings, Collages, Paintings, Sculptures and Constructions, 1916–1968*, Grosvenor Gallery, London.
Exhibited in *Collection Marguerite Arp-Hagenbach*, Kunstmuseum Basel.

1971
Exhibited in *The Non-Objective World, 1924–1939*, Galerie Jean Chauvelin, Paris. Exhibition toured to Annely Juda Fine Art, London, and Galleria Milano, Milan.

1972
Exhibited in *The Non-Objective World, 1939–1955*, Annely Juda Fine Art, London. Exhibition toured to Galerie Liatowitsch, Basel, and Galleria Milano, Milan.
Exhibited in *Geometric Abstraction: 1926–1942*, Dallas Museum of Fine Arts, Dallas.

1973
Exhibited in *The Non-Objective World, 1914–1955*, Annely Juda Fine Art, London. Exhibition toured to University of Texas Art Museum, Austin, Texas.

1978
Exhibited in Abstraction-Création, *1931–1936*, Westfälisches Landesmuseum für Kunst und Kulturgeschichte, Münster, Germany, and Musée d'art moderne de la Ville de Paris.

1980
Solo exhibition, *Paule Vézelay: Paintings, Drawings and Constructions, 1933–1980*, Zabriskie Gallery, New York.

1983
Solo exhibition, *Paule Vézelay*, The Tate Gallery, London.
Interviewed by Germaine Greer for the BBC series *Women of our Century*.

1984
20 March, death of Paule Vézelay.

1987
Solo exhibition, *Paule Vézelay: Paintings and Constructions*, Annely Juda Fine Art, London.

1988
Solo exhibition, *Paule Vézelay: Early Work, 1909–1939*, Michael Parkin Gallery, London, touring to Arnolfini Gallery, Bristol.
Solo exhibition, *Paule Vézelay: Imagination, Mathematics and Balance*, Zabriskie Gallery, New York.
Solo exhibition, *Paule Vézelay: Master of Line*, England & Co., London.
Included in *The Non-Objective World Revisited*, Annely Juda Fine Art, London.

1989
Solo exhibition, *Paule Vézelay: 1892–1984*, Roberts/Rutherston, London.
Solo exhibition, *Paule Vézelay & André Masson, Paintings and Works on Paper 1928–1934*, England & Co., London.

1991
Solo exhibition, *Paule Vézelay*, England & Co., London.

1993
Included in *Surrealism: Revolution by Night*, National Gallery of Australia, Canberra (also Queensland Art Gallery, Brisbane, and Art Gallery of New South Wales, Sydney).

1995
Joint exhibition, *Paule Vézelay / Hans Arp. The Enchantments of Purity*, Henry Moore Institute, Leeds.

1997
Solo exhibition, *Paule Vézelay: Early Figurative Works*, Abbot Hall Art Gallery, Kendal.

1998
Solo exhibition, *Paule Vézelay: Permit Denied*, Imperial War Museum, London.

2000
Solo exhibition, *Paule Vézelay: 1892–1984 Retrospective*, England & Co., London.

2002
Included in *Paris: Capital of the Arts 1900–1968*, Royal Academy of Arts, London, and Guggenheim Museum, Bilbao.

2003
Solo exhibition, *Paule Vézelay: Textiles and Textile Designs from the 1950s*, England & Co., London.

2004

Solo exhibition, *Paule Vézelay: 1892–1984 Retrospective*, England & Co., London.
Solo exhibition, *Lines in Space: Paule Vézelay & Linda Karshan*, England & Co., London.

2007

Joint exhibition, *Paule Vézelay and her Circle: Paris & the South of France*, England & Co., London.

2011

Included in *Modern British Sculpture*, Royal Academy of Arts, London.

2012

Solo exhibition, *Paule Vézelay: Abstraction-Création and Le Groupe Espace*, England & Co., London.
Included in *Designing Women: Post-War British Textiles*, Fashion and Textile Museum, London.

2016

Solo exhibition, *Paule Vézelay: Spotlight Display*, Tate Britain, London.

2021

Joint exhibition, *Paule Vézelay / Louise Hopkins*, 42 Carlton Place, Glasgow.
Included in *Parisian Abstracts. Abstraction-Création*, Modem Center for Modern & Contemporary Art, Debrecen, Hungary.

2023

Included in *Surréalisme au féminin?*, Musée de Montmartre, Paris

2025

Solo exhibition, *Paule Vézelay: Living Lines*, Royal West of England Academy, Bristol, and Towner Eastbourne.

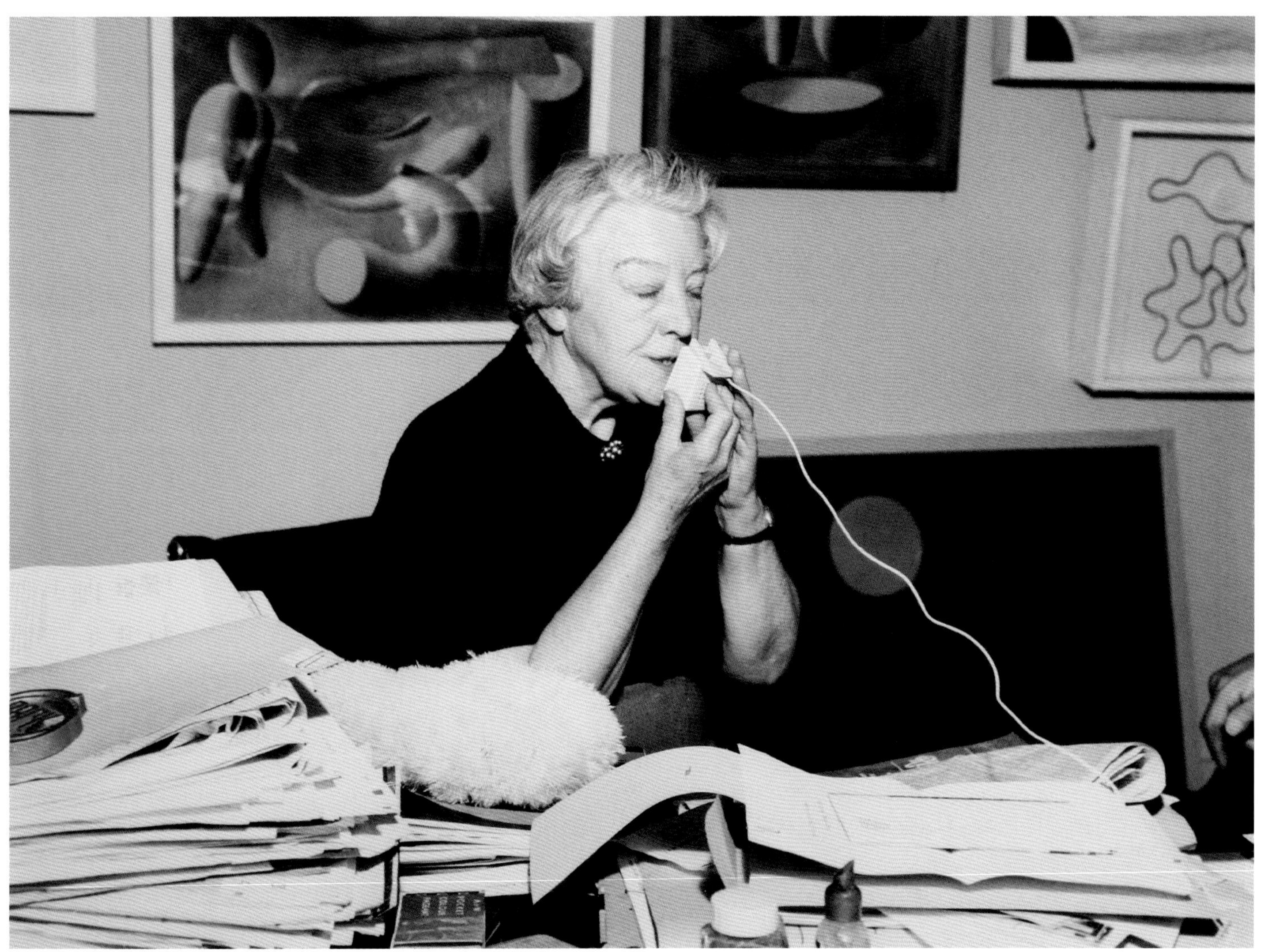

72
Paule Vézelay dictating notes, London, c.1970s,
photograph, Estate of Paule Vézelay

Notes

Introduction
Simon Grant

1 Paule Vézelay, 'Comment written for the Tate Gallery catalogue', 5 January 1964, Tate Archive, TGA 20002/8/2/1.
2 Paule Vézelay, 'Comment written for the Tate Gallery catalogue'.
3 Paule Vézelay talking to Germaine Greer, *Women of our Century. Paule Vézelay*, BBC TV, broadcast 27 July 1984.

Chapter 1. The Making of an International Artist
Simon Grant

1 Carl Einstein, quoted in Tom Holert, *Neolithic Childhood – Art in a False Present, c. 1930*, Diaphanes AG, 2018, p.287.
2 Charles Spencer, 'Talking to Paule Vézelay', *London Magazine*, vol.8, no.7, October 1969, p.69.
3 Unpublished text written c.1922, Estate of Paule Vézelay.
4 'Margaret Morris: Inspiring Champion of the Avant-Garde', *The Herald*, 8 July 2018.
5 'Wonderful Bathing Among the Attractions at Cap d'Antibes', *Daily Mail*, 8 September 1925.
6 Quoted in Sarah Wilson's text for *Paule Vézelay & André Masson: Paintings and Works on Paper*, exh.cat., England & Co., London, 1989.
7 Paule Vézelay to Ithell Colquhoun, 27 January 1934, Tate Archive, TGA 929/1/1/2303.
8 B.J. Kospoth, *The Chicago Tribune and the Daily News*, New York, 6 May 1928.
9 Paule Vézelay to Oliver Brown, 17 February 1954, Tate Archive, TGA 20002/1/1/2004.
10 Cited in André Masson, *Les Années Surréalistes: Correspondence 1916–1942*, La Manufacture, Paris, 1990, p.526, from an unpublished letter by Paule Vézelay to Gertrude Stein, c.1930, in the Beinecke Rare Book and Manuscript Library, Yale University, YCAL MSS 76, Series II.
11 Paule Vézelay, unpublished text, 1933, Tate Archive TGA 9027/1/2/1.
12 G. Grigson, 'Comment on England', *Axis*, vol.1 (January 1935), p.8.
13 Draft for 'Sophie Taeuber-Arp' by Paule Vézelay, written in Paris 1948, Tate Archive, TGA20002/14/2/21.
14 Sophie Taeuber-Arp to Paule Vézelay, 24 October 1938, Tate Archive, TGA20002/1/1/129.
15 Jean Arp, 'A Portrait of Sophie Taeuber-Arp', published in *Sophie Taeuber-Arp*, Musée National d'Art Moderne, Paris, 1964.
16 Quoted in James Thrall Soby (ed.), *Arp*, Museum of Modern Art, New York, 1958, p.15.
17 Paule Vézelay, 'Comments on *Lines in Space* – recherches en trois dimensions, tableaux de fils et ficelles tendus', January 1964, Tate Archive, TGA 8615/1.
18 Marguerite Hagenbach to Paule Vézelay, 10 August 1951, quoting Herta Wescher in *Nazional Zeitung Basel*, 7 August 1951, Tate Archive, TGA 20002/1/1/129.

Chapter 2. 'And I Dance'
Gemma Brace

1 Arthur Rimbaud, quoted in Paule Vézelay, 'Preface', *Recent Works by Paule Vézelay*, exh.cat. Alex Reid & Lefevre, Ltd. (Lefevre Galleries), London, 1942. Vézelay's quote is in the original French: 'J'ai tendu des cordes de clocher à clocher; des guirlandes de fenêtre à fenêtre; des chaines d'or d'étoile à étoile, et je danse.' From *Phrases* in *Les Illuminations* (1886). The English translation is taken from Wallace Fowlie, *Rimbaud's Illuminations: A Study in Angelism*, Camelot Press, London, 1953.
2 Sarah Wilson, 'Paule Vézelay at the Tate, Victor Willing at Kettle's Yard', *Artscribe International*, no.40, April 1983, p.50.
3 Paule Vézelay, 'Comment written for the Tate Gallery catalogue', 5 January 1964, Tate Archive, TGA 20002/8/2/1.
4 Paule Vézelay, 'Basic Elements in the Science of Drawing and Composition', Tate Archive, TGA20002/8/1/1.
5 Vézelay, 'Comment written for the Tate Gallery catalogue'.
6 Paule Vézelay, *Imagination, Mathematics, Balance*, 1975, Tate Archive, TGA 9027/1/25.
7 ibid.
8 Paule Vézelay, typewritten notes: 'Memoir by Marjorie Watson-Williams (the artist Paule Vézelay) 1892–1984: Childhood and student days', written August 1974, Estate of Paule Vézelay.
9 Marjorie Watson-Williams, 'Let Nothing be Lost Upon You', *Drawing and Design*, N.S., no.24, April 1922.
10 Typewritten copy of Tate Gallery catalogue entry for *Pont Neuf, Paris* (1921), PR313, Estate of Paule Vézelay.
11 Paule Vézelay, 'Cirque', produced c.1920–45, Estate of Paule Vézelay.
12 Sarah Wilson, 'Paule Vézelay: Harlequin and Columbine', *Paule Vézelay. Early Work 1909–1939*, exh.cat., Michael Parkin Fine Art, London, 1988.
13 Wilson, 'Paule Vézelay at the Tate', pp 50–51.
14 Paule Vézelay, typewritten notes: 'Thoughts on Pictorial Composition', undated, Estate of Paule Vézelay.
15 Paule Vézelay, 'Imagination', 1946, Estate of Paule Vézelay.
16 Paule Vézelay, 'Juan Gris: 1987–1927', *Artwork*, vol.4, no.16, winter 1928.
17 Ronald Alley, *Paule Vézelay. Paintings and Constructions*, exh.cat., Annely Juda Fine Art, London, 1987.
18 Sarah Wilson, 'Paule Vézelay: A Biography', *Imagination, Mathematics, Balance*, exh.cat., Zabriskie Gallery, New York, 1988.
19 Sarah Wilson, *Paule Vézelay and André Masson. Paintings and Works on Paper, 1928–1934*, exh. cat., England & Co., London, 1989, p.6.
20 Virginia Pitts Rembert, 'Paule Vézelay's Lines in Space and Other Works', *Arts Magazine*, vol.55, November 1930, pp 83–103.
21 Sarah Wilson, 'Imagination, Mathematics, Balance', *Imagination, Mathematics, Balance*, exh.cat., Zabriskie Gallery, New York, 1988.
22 Paule Vézelay, quoted in Sarah Wilson, *Paule Vézelay/Hans Arp: The Enchantments of Purity*, exh.cat., Henry Moore Institute, Leeds, 1995, p.4.
23 J.P. Hodin, 'Paule Vézelay: Master of Classical Abstraction', article partly published in *Contemporary Artists* 1977, full typewritten article, Estate of Paule Vézelay.
24 William Lipke, 'Paule Vézelay', 1965, Tate Archive, TGA9027/2/5.
25 The English translation is 'Research in Three Dimensions: Pictures with Wire and String'.
26 Vézelay, 'Comment written for the Tate Gallery catalogue'.
27 Paule Vézelay, 'Meandering with Two Mediums' (also known in other versions as 'Meandering with Mediums'), 1970, Estate of Paule Vézelay.
28 Paule Vézelay, quoted in Leslie Harcourt, *Paule Vézelay, Master of Line*, exh.cat., England & Co., London, 1988.
29 Anatole France, quoted by Paule Vézelay in Chapter 8, 'Primary Elements and the Vézelay Code of Centralisation in Pictorial Composition', *Basic Elements in the Science of Drawing and Composition*, Paule Vézelay Archive, Tate, TGA20002/8/1/1.

Chapter 3. Textile Designs
Helen Janecek

1 Paule Vézelay talking to Germaine Greer, *Women of our Century. Paule Vézelay*, BBC TV, broadcast 27 July 1984.
2 'Et le point du vue architectural commande tout, votre projet n'est d'ailleurs pas suffisamment architectural, comme d'ailleurs ceux de Kandinsky dont Madame Bucher vous fut voir la réalisation sur tissu.' Jean Bauret to Vézelay, unpublished letter, 16 February 1945, Paule Vézelay Collection, Tate Archive, TGA 20002/3/2/2/1.
3 Société Industrielle de la Lys fabric samples, Tate Archive, TGA 20002/3/4/1-3; and photographs, Tate Archive, TGA 20002/3/1/10-15.
4 Vézelay to Zika Ascher, unpublished letter, 24 September 1945, Tate Archive, TGA 20002/3/2/1/11.
5 Valerie D. Mendes and Frances Hinchcliffe, 'Fabric for Fashion', in *Ascher: Fabric. Art. Fashion*, exh.cat., Victoria & Albert Museum, London, 1987, p.96.
6 Richard Chamberlain, 'Textile Design', in *Austerity to Affluence. British Art & Design 1945–1962*, exh.cat., Fine Art Society, London, 1997, pp 33–7. On the effect of the exhibition on British artists, see also Geoffrey Rayner, Richard Chamberlain and Anne-Marie Stapleton, 'The 1960s', *Artists' Textiles 1940–1976*, Merrell Holberton/Fine Art Society, London, 1997, p.88.
7 See 'Spring in the Home', *The Sketch*, 21 April 1954 (copy in the Tate Archive: TGA 20002/3/5); and Vézelay to Heal's, unpublished letter, 25 April 1956, Tate Archive, TGA 20002/3/2/3/47.
8 Matteo de Leeuw-de Monti, 'Sonia Delaunay – the Designs for Metz & Co', in Anne Montfort and Cécile Godefroy (eds), *Sonia Delaunay*, exh.cat., Tate Modern, London, 2015, pp 164–81.

9 Vézelay to Worthington, unpublished letter, 4 April 1953, Tate Archive, TGA 20002/3/2/4/18.
10 Vézelay to Worthington, unpublished letter, 26 May 1954, Tate Archive, TGA 20002/3/2/3/8.
11 Chamberlain, 'Textile Design', pp 33–7.
12 Andrew Casey, *Lucienne Day: In the Spirit of the Age*, Antique Collectors' Club, Woodbridge (Suffolk), 2014, p.65.
13 Paule Vézelay talking to Germaine Greer, *Women of our Century. Paule Vézelay*, BBC TV, broadcast 27 July 1984.
14 Vézelay to Worthington, unpublished and undated letter, Tate Archive, TGA 20002/3/2/3/161.
15 Worthington to Vézelay, unpublished letter, 7 February 1963, Tate Archive, TGA 20002/3/2/3/148.
16 Gordon Russell, 'The Industrial Designer', *Art in Industry*, vol.1, no.1 no date, pp 5–10.
17 Worthington to Vézelay, unpublished letter, 22 June 1956, Tate Archive, TGA 20002/3/2/3/51.
18 Worthington to Vézelay, unpublished letter, 26 July 1956, Tate Archive, TGA 20002/3/2/3/55.
19 Vézelay to Worthington, unpublished letters, 17 March to 18 May 1969, Tate Archive, TGA 20002/3/2/3/201, 203, 204, 205, 206.
20 Rayner, Chamberlain and Stapleton, 'The 1960s', p.226.
21 See, respectively, Vézelay to Worthington, unpublished letter, 17 March 1956, Tate Archive, TGA 20002/3/2/3/43; and Vézelay to Worthington, unpublished letter, 16 July 1956, Tate Archive, TGA 20002/3/2/3/53.
22 Ngozu Ikoku, 'Paule Vézelay's textiles and the rise of modern non-figurative design', *The Decorative Arts Society Journal*, vol.44, 2020, pp 70–86.
23 Anon., 'Textile designs inspired by paintings', *Furnishing World & Carpets and Soft Furnishing Weekly*, 7 August 1959, pp 29–30.
24 Worthington to Vézelay, unpublished letter, 10 February 1961, Tate Archive, TGA 20002/3/2/3/118.
25 Penny Sparke, 'Conclusion', in Penny Sparke (ed.), *Did Britain Make It? British Design in Context 1946–86*, Design Council, London, 1986, pp 165–7.
26 Paule Vézelay talking to Germaine Greer, *Women of our Century. Paule Vézelay*, BBC TV, broadcast 27 July 1984.
27 Vézelay quoted in Anon., 'Textile designs inspired by paintings' *Furnishing World*, 7 August 1959, pp 29–30..

Chapter 4. Decades of Self-Reinvention
Sarah Wilson

Note: All unpublished texts quoted are from Vézelay's archives, Estate of Paule Vézelay, Winchester, consulted 10 January 2018, courtesy of the late Sally Jarman.

1 *Paule Vézelay. Paintings, Drawings and Constructions, 1933–1980*, New York, Virginia Zabriskie, 1980.
2 See Sarah Wilson, 'Abstraction-Création and the London/Paris axis: a personal comment', in Flóra Mészáros (ed.), *Parisian Abstracts, International Hungarians and Abstraction-Création*, Modem, Debrecen, Hungary, 2021, pp 104–16.
3 Former Tate curator Richard Morphet, in an email to the author, 10 April 2024.
4 It is important to distinguish use of the term 'School of Paris'/'École de Paris' by Anglo-American participants and a pre-war 'École de Paris' defined by immigration linked to Jewish minorities and pogroms in Russia and eastern Europe.
5 For my texts on Vézelay, Moss, Fahrelnissa Zeid, Nadia Khodossievich, Françoise Gilot and Niki de Saint Phalle, see http://sarah-wilson.london/index.html#index.
6 In the typescript 'Pictorial Composition' (1978), Estate of Paule Vézelay, she refers to Whistler's *Gentle Art of Making Enemies*, 1890.
7 Paule Vézelay talking to Germaine Greer, *Women of our Century. Paule Vézelay*, BBC TV broadcast 27 July 1984. Research, Sarah Wilson.'
8 Saml. Pepys, Jnr (R. M. Freeman and Robert A. Bennett) *A Diary of the Great Warr*, with effigies by M. Watson-Williams, John Lane, London, 1916.
9 Information on Léon de Smet from the Christie's notice for *Mlle Watson-Williams*, 1918, Sale: London, 20 October 1988, no.114; Witt Library, The Courtauld, University of London.
10 The untitled reproduction of de Smet's full-length portrait, *Miss M. Watson Williams*, in the Witt Library, stamped '1975', is also labelled 'Ex-Cornish collection. Pres. to Hampstead Public Library, 1928'.
11 Vézelay: 'As an art student, I hunted for Staffordshire china figures, Japanese prints and old profiles and silhouettes'. 'Silhouette, collage and pastel', author's typescript, marked 'Leonardo, Log no.F5, edited draft . . . Received 4 August 1970'.
12 See *Mlle Watson-Williams*, 1918, in Émile Langui, *Léon de Smet*, Léon de Smet Museum, Deurle, 1976, p. 35.
13 Paule Vézelay, typescript, 'Meandering with Pastel, Silhouette and Collage', 1970, Estate of Paule Vézelay.
14 Léon de Smet, *Femme nue allongée*, Christie's sale, 1 December 1981, no 136. Witt Library. De Smet may conceivably have painted her head on a model's body.
15 See Jean-Louis Cohen, Guillemette Morel Journel (eds), *Paris moderne, 1914–1945*, Gallimard, Paris, 2023.
16 Lucy Howarth's definitive PhD precedes her Marlow Moss retrospective, Museumhaus Konstruktiv, Zurich, 2017; and Lucy Howarth, *Marlow Moss*, Eiderdown Books, 2019.
17 See Tirza True Latimer, *Women Together/ Women Apart. Portraits of Lesbian Paris*, Rutgers University Press, New Jersey, 2005; Jane Alison and Coralie Malissard, *Modern Couples, Art Intimacy and the Avant-garde*, Barbican Art Gallery, London, 2018; and Camille Morineau and Lucia Pesapane, *Pionnières. Artistes dans le Paris des années folles*, Musée du Luxembourg, Paris, 2022.
18 See Sarah Wilson, 'Introduction', in *Paule Vézelay and André Masson. Paintings and Works on Paper, 1928–1934*, England & Co., London, 1989.
19 See also Giacometti, 'Objets mobiles et muets', *Le Surréalisme su service de la révolution* 3, December 1931, pp 18–19.
20 Roger Caillois, 'La Mante religieuse', *Minotaure*, no.5, 1934, pp 23–6. See the handwritten marginal note to the (late) typescript 'Escargots': 'Before bringing her young into the world she has to kill and devour her mate.' In 'Chastity' (see below, note 25) Vézelay refers to Jean-Henri Fabre (*Souvenirs entomologiques*, Paris, 1897; *Social Life in the Insect World*, Pelican, London, 1937).
21 Paule Vézelay, typescript, 'Sophie Arp', 1948, Estate of Paule Vézelay.
22 Paule Vézelay talking to Germaine Greer, *Women of our Century. Paule Vézelay*, BBC TV, broadcast 27 July 1984.
23 *Paule Vézelay. Oeuvres de 1928 à 1946*, Galerie Colette Allendy, 1946-7, with her text 'Imagination, Mathématiques et Équilibre'.
24 See the free-verse poem *Ascona*, ending 'I hold this moment of peace to my aching heart', no date, handwritten manuscript, ink.
25 The St George's Gallery show was prefaced by the Surrealist poet and filmmaker Humphrey Jennings. See Jean Arp, *Fabliaux sombres* (*Fables of Darkness*), signed Jean Arp Meudon, 1949, translated by Ben Jarman, 1987, Estate of Paule Vézelay; and Sarah Wilson, *Paule Vézelay/Hans Arp. The Enchantments of Purity*, exh.cat., Henry Moore Institute, Leeds, 1995, n.p.
26 'Chastity' (undated typescript) was withheld from the Tate archives. It mixes references from Ludwig Goldscheider (*Etruscan Sculpture*, Phaidon, London, 1941) and Fabre's praying mantis with issues of 'concupiscence', prostitution, the unmarried mother, birth control and abortion; with handwritten references to John Stuart Mill, Mary Wollstonecraft and Emily Brontë . . . and an acute sense of injustice and pain. A reference to Etruscan sculpture in 'Turn a blind eye' (typescript dated September 1956) encourages a 1950s date.
27 I visited Vézelay in order to write: 'Paule Vézelay at the Tate, Victor Willing in Kettle's Yard', *Artscribe*, no.40, April 1983, pp 50–52.
28 'As I lie here / my torpid gaze meanders all around . . .' The subtext of Vézelay's post-war writing experiments are at odds with her Romantic-era free verse and vocabulary.
29 See her letter to the editor of *Leonardo*, Frank J. Malina, 12 November 1970, complaining about the over-editing of her subsequently unpublished article (presumably 'Meandering with Pastel, Silhouette and Collage' – see above, note 12).
30 See correspondence dated 1975 in Tate's entry for *White Shapes in Movement* (1930): https://www.tate.org.uk/art/artworks/vezelay-white-shapes-in-movement-l03890.
31 Germaine Greer is referring to her book *The Obstacle Race: The Fortunes of Women Painters and their work*, Secker and Warburg, London, 1979.

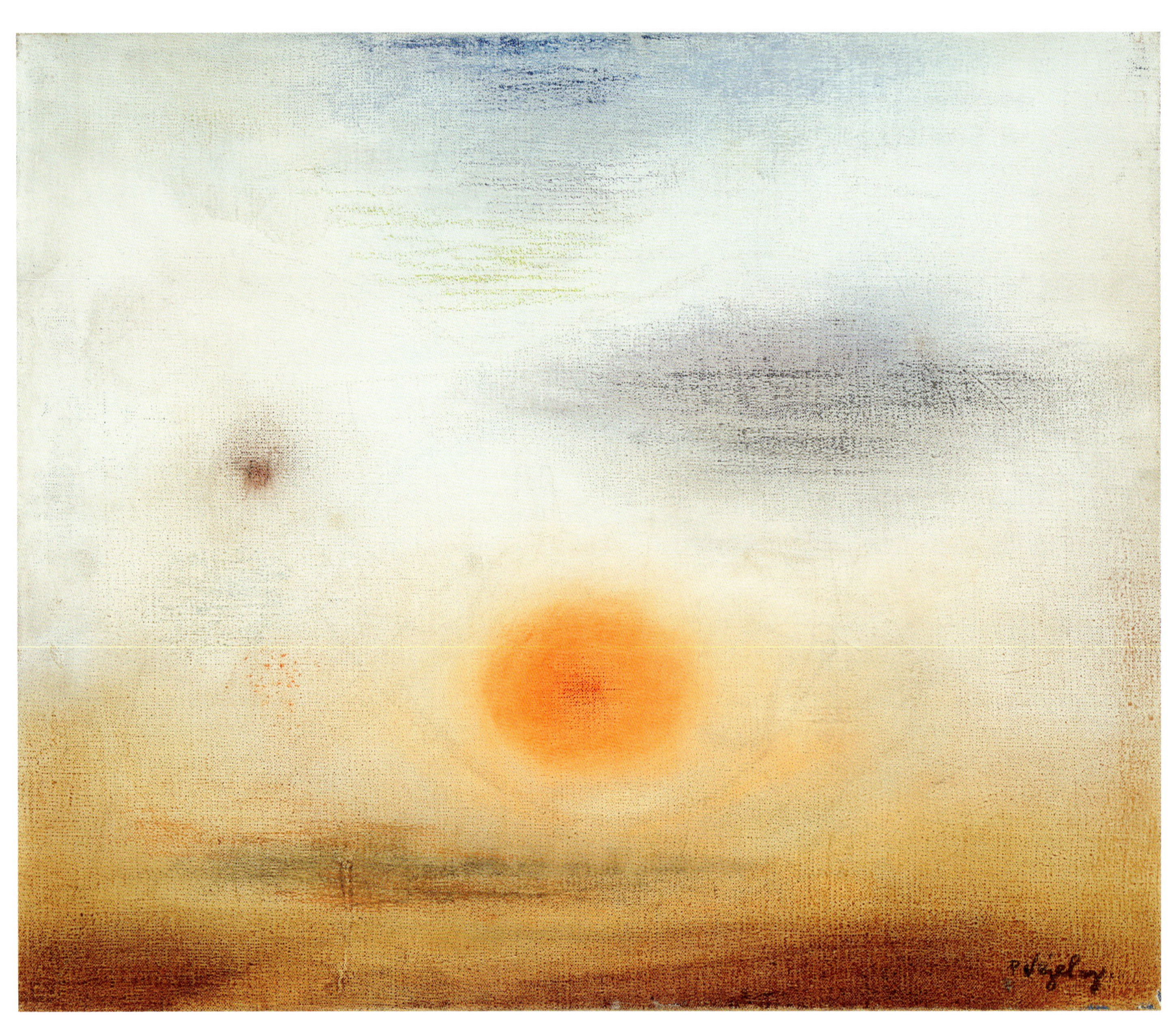

73
Paule Vézelay, *Light and Space*, 1978,
pastel, 46 × 38 cm, Estate of Paule Vézelay

Select Bibliography

Alley, Ronald, *The Foreign Paintings, Drawings and Sculpture*, Tate Gallery, London, 1959

Alley, Ronald, *Catalogue of the Tate Gallery Collection of Modern Art Other Than Works by British Artists*, Tate Gallery, London, 1981

Alley, Ronald, *Paule Vézelay*, Tate Gallery, London, 1983

Alley, Ronald, *Paule Vézelay: Paintings and Constructions*, exh.cat., Annely Juda Fine Art, London, 1987

Anon., 'Paule Vézelay's Textile Designs Inspired by Paintings', *Furnishing World*, August 1957, pp 29–30

Baker, Harriet, 'The Living Lines of Paule Vézelay', *Apollo*, https://www.apollo-magazine.com/the-living-lines-of-paule-vezelay/, May 2017

Bénézit, Emmanuel, *Dictionnaire critique et documentaire des peintres, sculpteurs, dessinateurs et graveurs*, vol.10, Paris, 1976

Braun, A.A., 'An Old Master of the Future', *Drawing and Design*, April 1922

Brion, Marcel, *Paule Vézelay: Lines in Space and Their Shadows 1936–1954*, exh.cat., Ernest Brown & Phillips, Leicester Galleries, London, 1954

Brion, Marcel, *Art abstrait*, Albin Michel, Paris, 1956

Caldicott, Léonie, *Paule Vézelay: Women of our Century*, BBC Books, London, 1984

Campbell, Louise, *Studio Lives. Architect, Art and Artist in 20th-Century Britain*, Lund Humphries, 2019

Cumming, Laura, 'Surface Work', in *The Guardian*, 15 April 2018

Desnos, Robert, *Paule Vézelay*, exh.cat., Galerie Vavin-Raspail, Paris, 1930

Estienne, Charles, 'Les Arts', in *Combat*, 2 June 1946

Fowler, Alan, 'A Forgotten British Constructivist Group: The London Branch of Groupe Espace, 1953–59', *The Burlington Magazine*, vol.149, no.1248, March 2007, pp 173–9

Foster, Alicia, *Tate Women Artists*, Tate Publishing, London, 2014

Greer, Germaine, 'Women of our Century: Paule Vézelay', *The Listener*, 2 August 1984

Grieve, Alastair, 'This is Tomorrow, a Remarkable Exhibition Born from Contention', *The Burlington Magazine*, vol.136, no.1093, April 1994, pp 225–32

Harcourt, Leslie, *Paule Vézelay Master of Line*, exh. cat., England & Co., London, 1988

Howarth, Lucy, *Marlow Moss (1889–1958)*, PhD thesis, University of Plymouth, 2008

Hodin, J.P., 'Paule Vézelay: Master of Classical Abstraction', unpublished and undated text, Estate of Paule Vézelay

Jackson, Lesley, *Material: Textile. Modern British Female Designers*, Messum's, 2020

Jarman, Sally, 'Marjorie Watson-Williams', *Oxford Dictionary of National Biography*, Oxford University Press, 2004

Jennings, Humphrey, *Paule Vézelay*, exh.cat., St George's Gallery, London, 1949

Kospoth, B.J., 'Paule Vézelay's Paintings', *The Chicago Tribune and the Daily News*, 6 May 1928

Levaillant, Françoise (ed.), *André Masson: les années surréalistes: correspondence 1916–1942*, La Manufacture, Paris, 1990, pp 524–34

Lipke, William, 'Paule Vézelay', 1965, Tate Archive, TGA9027/2/5

Lipke, William, 'Paule Vézelay at Grosvenor Gallery', *Studio International*, no.176, 1968

Marano, Virginia, 'Living forms: Paule Vézelay's Encounter with Alberto Giacometti's Surrealist Objects', Art UK online, https://artuk.org/discover/stories/living-forms-paule-vezelays-encounter-with-alberto-giacomettis-surrealist-objects, 2021

McIntyre, Raymond, 'Two Concepts of a Circus', *Architectural Review*, vol.68, 1930

Nash, Paul, *Paule Vézelay*, exh.cat., Lefevre Galleries, London, 1936

Naylor, Colin, and Genesis P-Orridge (eds), *Contemporary Artists*, St Martin's Press, New York, 1977

Osborne, Harold (ed.), *The Oxford Companion to Twentieth Century Art*, Oxford University Press, 1981

Sabacek, Jiri, 'Paule Vézelay', *Sculpture International*, vol.2, no.4 (April 1969), pp 40–44

Seuphor, Michel, *A Dictionary of Abstract Painting*, Methuen, 1958

Seuphor, Michel, *The Sculpture of this Century: Dictionary of Modern Sculpture*, George Braziller Inc., New York, 1959

Seuphor, Michel, *L'art abstrait 2: 1918–1938*, Maeght Editeur, Paris, 1972

Spencer, Charles, 'Talking to Paule Vézelay', *London Magazine*, vol.8, no.7 (October 1969), pp 69–75

Taeuber-Arp, Sophie (ed.), *Plastique*, no.2, Summer 1937

Taylor, Brendan, and Alan Fowler, *Elements of Abstraction: Space, Line and Interval in Modern British Art*, Southampton City Art Gallery, 2006

Vézelay, Paule, 'Juan Gris: 1987–1927', *Artwork*, vol.4, no.16, Winter 1928

Vézelay, Paule, 'Preface', *Recent Works by Paule Vézelay*, exh.cat., Alex Reid & Lefevre Ltd., London, 1942

Weiner, Eric, *Paule Vézelay: Drawings and Constructions 1933–1980*, exh.cat., Zabriskie Gallery, New York, 1980

Wescher, Herta, *Collage*, Harry N. Abrams, New York, 1968

Wilson, Sarah, 'Paule Vézelay at Tate, Victor Willing at Kettle's Yard', *Artscribe International*, no.40 (April 1983), p.51

Wilson, Sarah 'Paule Vézelay: Harlequin and Columbine', *Paule Vézelay Early Work 1909–1939*, exh.cat., Michael Parkin Fine Art, London, 1988

Wilson, Sarah, 'Paule Vézelay: A Biography', *Imagination, Mathematics, Balance*, Zabriskie Gallery, New York, 1988

Wilson, Sarah, *Paule Vézelay and André Masson. Paintings and Works on Paper, 1928–1934*, exh. cat., England & Co., London, 1989

Wilson, Sarah, *Paule Vézelay / Hans Arp: The Enchantment of Purity*, exh.cat., Henry Moore Institute, Leeds, 1995

Wilson, Sarah, *Paule Vézelay: A Retrospective*, exh.cat., England & Co., London 2000

Wilson, Sarah, *Paule Vézelay and Her Circle: Paris and the South of France*, exh.cat., England & Co., London, 2007

Zervos, Christian, 'Les expositions à Paris et ailleurs: Paule Vézelay', *Cahiers d'art*, vol.9, 1934, p.256

Editor's note: Paule Vézelay published many articles and texts as Marjorie Watson-Williams from 1917–22 and as Paule Vézelay from 1928–77. Her extensive archive is held at Tate, with further material held by the Estate.

Works in Public Collections

UK

Arts Council of Great Britain
Bath, Victoria Art Gallery
Belfast, Ulster Museum
Bolton Art Gallery
Bradford University
Bristol Museum and Art Gallery
Chichester, Pallant House Gallery
Derby Museum and Art Gallery
Eastbourne, Towner Art Gallery
Edinburgh, Scottish National Gallery of Modern Art
Kendal, Abbot Hall Art Gallery
Lancaster University
Leeds Art Gallery
Leeds, Henry Moore Institute
Liverpool University
London, Tate
London, British Museum
London, Imperial War Museum
London, National Portrait Gallery
London, Victoria & Albert Museum
London, Department of the Environment
Newcastle upon Tyne, Laing Art Gallery
Norwich, University of East Anglia (Collection of Constructivist Art and Design)
Oxford, Ashmolean Museum

France

Grenoble, Musée de Grenoble
Pantin, Centre National des Arts Plastiques
Paris, Musée National d'Art Moderne, Centre Pompidou
Rennes, Musée des Beaux-Arts de Rennes
Saint-Étienne, Musée d'Art Moderne et Contemporain
Vézelay, Christian & Yvonne Zervos Association

Worldwide

Australia, Canberra, National Gallery of Australia
Portugal, Lisbon, Contemporary Art Museum – Centro Cultural de Belém
Switzerland, Basel, Kunstmuseum

Acknowledgements

The Estate of Paule Vézelay have warmly supported this project at every turn, at first courtesy of Paule Vézelay's niece, the late Sally Jarman, and now her son and granddaughter, Sam Jarman and Kanako Jarman.

The Royal West of England Academy in Bristol are delighted to launch this exhibition in the very same building in which Vézelay studied art as a young woman. Special thanks are due to curator and writer Gemma Brace, former Head of Exhibitions at the RWA, for shaping this exhibition project in its earliest stages.

For their expert knowledge and championship of Vézelay's work, the contributions of Professor Sarah Wilson and Jane England, Director of England & Co. Gallery, are much appreciated.

This book is supported by a Publications Grant from the Paul Mellon Centre for Studies in British Art.

We are also indebted to James Trotman for his generous support, which has enabled this book to be published.

We express our thanks to all those at Lund Humphries who have brought this book to fruition, in particular Lucy Myers, Lucy Clark, Sarah Thorowgood and Rebeccah Williams.

We extend sincere thanks to all those individuals and organisations who have made this book and the accompanying exhibition possible, by lending their expertise, time and, in many cases, treasured works of art:

Jonathan W Anderson
Piet Boyens
Sara Cooper, Towner Eastbourne
Christian Derouet
Richard Emerson
Jane England, England & Co.
Amy Fairley, Perth Museum
Caroline Fournillon-Courant, Musée Zervos, Vézelay, France
Heloisa Becker Genish
Adrian Glew, Tate Archive
Steve Gorton
Marcus Halliwell, MacConnal-Mason Gallery, London
Janet Hardie, Bonhams
Katy Hessel
Jennifer Higgie
Tom Holert
Richard Ingleby
Kathryn Johnson, Royal West of England Academy, Bristol
Walburga Krupp
Sarah Murray, Leeds Museums and Galleries
Sacha Llewellyn
Frances Morris
Sarah Norris, Pallant House Gallery, Chichester
Catherine Petitgas
Ruth Seager
Natalia Sidlina
Robin de Smet
Polly Staple, Tate
Maike Steinkamp, Stiftung Arp, Berlin, Germany
Lisa Stevenson, Sotheby's
Jana Teuscher, Stiftung Arp, Berlin, Germany
Edwin van Trijp, Oscar de Vos Gallery, Sint-Martens-Latem, Belgium
Jo Elsworth, University of Bristol Theatre Collection

And those wishing to remain anonymous.

Image Credits

Courtesy of Bonhams: 10
© 2014 Christie's Images Limited: 50, 54, 55
Courtesy of England & Co: frontispiece, 9, 18, 20, 27, 28, 30, 33, 34, 61, 67, 70
Courtesy of Lucy Haworth: 56
Courtesy François Jay. © François Jay: 11
Kunstmuseum Basel. Gift of Hans Arp: 14
Liss Llewellyn: 35
Courtesy Marlborough Fine Art, London: 4
National Galleries of Scotland. Purchased with the support of The National Lottery Heritage Fund and Art Fund, 1995 © ADAGP, Paris and DACS, London 2024: 60
National Portrait Gallery, London: 1
Pallant House Gallery, Chichester, (Donated in Memory of Khaled Al Bahar 2022): 48
RWA Collection: 26
Sotheby's: 51
Photo: Tate: 12, 15, 16, 57
Courtesy University of Bristol: 6

Index

Note: italic page numbers indicate figures; page numbers followed by n refer to notes.